THE
OXENHOLME
HOUNDS

When, Where, and How They Hunted
SEASON 1934-5

THE ILLUSTRATED DIARY OF HERMIONE DREW

Reproduced from the original by
Trevor Hughes

AMBERLEY

Dedication

I dedicate this book to Hermione Drew otherwise known as the
'Fat Drew', who had the foresight and skill to commit this account
of the Oxenholme Staghounds to paper.

Acknowledgements

Mr F. Downham, Mrs W. E. Taylor, Mr and Mrs J. Taylor, Mr & Mrs M. Heaton,
Mrs D. McAlpine, A. Heaton, Mrs Nancy Jones and Mrs Anthony Cropper.
Special thanks to Arthur Nicholls for all his help in researching information for this book.

First published 2009

Amberley Publishing Plc
Cirencester Road, Chalford,
Stroud, Gloucestershire, GL6 8PE
www.amberley-books.com

© Trevor Hughes, 2009

British Library Cataloguing in Publication Data.
A catalogue record for this book is available from the British Library.

ISBN 978 1 84868 608 3

Typesetting and origination by Amberley Publishing Plc
Printed in Great Britain

Foreword

This small booklet, detailing the adventures and mishaps of the Oxenholme Staghounds over a six-month period, is a time capsule of a long-lost era and is a fascinating social document of a now forbidden pastime. The accompanying paintings, which relate directly to the text, are beautifully crafted with great skill and much humour and bring to light, far better than any photograph, the atmosphere and camaraderie of that generation. Our grateful thanks must go to Hermione Drew who, as the author of this amazing document, proceeds to make fun of herself and the participants, graphically enacted, through the wonderful paintings and narrative. There were three Drew sisters of which I believe only two took part in the hunt. The family lived in Leasgill near Heversham.

The members of the Oxenholme Staghounds, featured in the narrative, were drawn from all the important families who lived in Kendal and the surrounding area. One only has to look at the list to see many well-known names, which are still around today. The Croppers of Burneside, the Crewdsons of Helm Lodge, the Somervells and the Heatons of Prizet to name but a few. As an interesting footnote, I discovered that Miss Ann Somervell, who I believe is the one mentioned in the narrative, was actually killed some time later in a riding accident. There is a full list of members mentioned in this narrative and where possible I have indicated where they lived. The Master of the Hounds in 1934 was Miss Weston who lived at Endmoor.

The original document, which was given to me by a relative, is now in the Cumbria Records Office to be kept for future generations to enjoy.

The Oxenholme Staghounds was finally finished at the start of the Second World War in 1939/40 and was never restarted. Contrary to popular belief, the hunt very rarely resulted in a kill and, as can be seen in the reported accounts later in this text, on many occasions the deer was actually brought in by local transport and released. Following the day's sport, the deer was then recaptured and transported back to safety. It is worth noting that the only kill recorded in this narrative was a stag, which had to be shot because it was injured.

The hunt operated over a very large area in Cumbria and Lancashire and covers Arnside, Farleton, Dallam, Grange-Over-Sands, the Lyth Valley, Milnthorpe, Natland, New Hutton, Oxenholme, Rigmaden, Silverdale, the Vale of Lune and Yealand.

Trevor Hughes

A LADY MASTER OF STAGHOUNDS.
Miss F. Weston, who has had
the Lunesdale and Oxenholme
Staghounds since 1930.

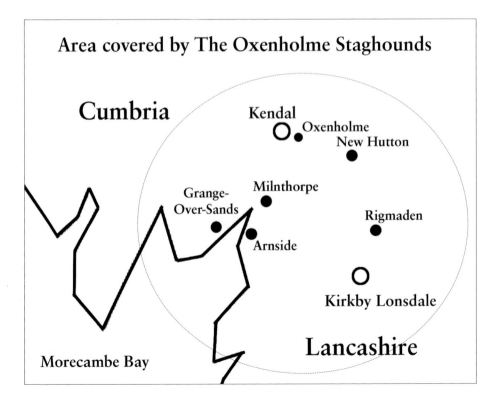

Area covered by The Oxenholme Staghounds

Cumbria

Kendal
Oxenholme
New Hutton

Grange-
Over-Sands
Milnthorpe

Rigmaden

Arnside

Kirkby Lonsdale

Lancashire

Morecambe Bay

Deer Hunting in Britain: Some Background Information

References:
Encyclopaedia Britannica vols 4/912 & 20/651
"Fox hunting was probably an adjunct to stag and deer hunting. The same hounds were used. The hounds were controlled by the Huntsman. The Master of the Hunt, the Huntsman and the Whipper-in took precedence over the other members of the Hunt. Hares were hunted using dogs known as harriers. Hunting was a national upper-class pastime. The day's hunting began with a Meet where the members acknowledged the Master and received hospitality from one of the members of the Meet as the host".

"Blood Sport – Hunting in Britain since 1066" by E. Griffin.

The provision of food in the earliest days was either by growing plants or hunting wild animals. By the 12th century the monarch had achieved dominance over his subjects and established royal deer parks. These were leased or rented out to reliable subjects and brought revenue to the monarch. Hunting as a sport as opposed for good became a royal prerogative. Huge sums were spent by the monarch on hunting. The aristocratic hunt involved fine clothes, ritual, music and a special language. When a deer was killed its head was held triumphantly before the returning party. Venison was a royal dish and the common people poached it to their peril. Food for the royal table took precedence over the morality of hunting. Titled and similar families set up their own private deer parks for hunting purposes. During the Civil War there was a campaign by the Puritans against blood sports but hunting survived. In the 17th century there was an increasing amount of deforestation and the private deer parks became a shadow of their former glory. The moral drive against hunting eventually failed but the world of hunting never fully recovered. Under the Restoration the monarch gave a decisive lead to hunting. Samuel Pepys wrote in his diary about a hunt in August 1666, "A great match of hunting of a Stagg the King had. ... The King tired of all their horses and came home with not above two or three able to keep pace with him." The King turned his attention to restoring the royal forests. Under the Hanoverians the Kings were less interested in hunting although George III loved it. They often secured tame animals which were brought to the hunt and set loose to be chased, rather than hunting wild deer. The deer were recaptured ready for a further future hunt. George IV had no interest in hunting, his interests led elsewhere in less manly pursuits. The future of royal hunting became uncertain. The country deer parks fell into a hopeless state of disrepair although some hunting still continued. With the Victorians there was a constant campaign against "cruel sports" and, with less deer to chase, foxhunting with harriers began to take the place of deer hunting – but stag hunting was still carried out in a few parts of the country.

Deer Stalking

"Deer stalking" is widely used among British and Irish sportsmen to signify almost all forms of sporting deer shooting – an expression that in Britain and Ireland which had historically been reserved exclusively for the sporting pursuit of deer with scent-seeking hounds, with unarmed followers typically on horseback. The vast majority of deer hunted in the UK are stalked. The phrase deer hunting, however, has also been used to refer (in England and Wales) to the traditional practice of chasing deer with packs of hounds, now illegal under the Hunting Act 2004. In the late nineteenth and twentieth centuries, there were several packs of staghounds hunting "carted deer" in England and Ireland. Carted deer were Red deer kept in captivity for the sole purpose of being hunted and recaptured alive.

Species of Deer

Of the six species of deer in the UK; Red deer, Roe deer, Fallow deer, Sika deer, Muntjac deer, and Chinese water deer, as well as hybrids of these deer, all have been hunted to a degree reflecting their relative population either as sport or for the purposes of culling. Closed seasons for deer vary by species and the practice of declaring a closed season in England dates back to medieval times, when it was called fence month and commonly lasted from 9 June to 9 July, though the actual dates varied. It is illegal to use bows to hunt any wild animal in the UK under the Wildlife and Countryside Act 1981. Victorian era dramatist W. S. Gilbert remarked, "Deer-stalking would be a very fine sport if only the deer had guns."

Hunting with Hounds

The way in which the red deer were hunted was for a character called the 'harbourer' to follow the intended quarry to the wood where it lay up for the night. In the morning, before the meet, the harbourer would carefully examine the perimeter of the wood to ensure that the stag had not left. After the harbourer had reported to the Master, the Huntsman would take about six hounds, called 'tufters', into the wood to rouse the intended quarry and start it running, separating it from any other deer that might be in the wood. This having been achieved, the tufters were taken back and the main pack were brought out and laid on the scent of the stag which, by now, would have had a good start. After a chase of indeterminate duration, the stag would become exhausted and would come to bay to face the hounds, often in water, where it would be shot at close range by one of the hunt servants. The practice of hunting with hounds, other than using two hounds to flush deer to be shot by waiting marksmen, has been banned in the UK since 2005.

The History of
The Oxenholme Staghounds

The History of The Oxenholme Staghounds

The history of the Oxenholme Staghounds is detailed in a couple of small booklets, one published in 1902 entitled *The Oxenholme Hunt* by C. J. C. and the other in 1923 entitled *The Lunesdale & Oxenholme Staghounds* by William Scarth-Dixon. The following are extracts from them.

The Oxenholme Hunt
by C. J. C.

I have been asked to write an account of the Oxenholme Hunt, which has now flourished for just about fifty years, and as the jubilee of the hunt is now approaching, it may not be amiss to record some outline of its history.

There has been hunting of one sort and another all through the last century, and probably for longer, in the valley of the Kent. A pack existed, known as the Kendal Hounds, but for what quarry they were kept is now buried in obscurity. It is recorded that there was a yearly meet on Helme, when the mayor of the town was elected, and doubtless a long dinner after the hunt, but all accurate records seem to have disappeared.

Harry Rauthmell had a pack of hounds at Hutton Bridge End from 1820 till well into the forties. They would hunt any thing they could find, though a fox was preferred. A run is recorded when they found in the Rigmaden covers and ran to Hutton Roof Crag, the fox getting to ground with the hounds in view. Harry Rauthmell was a very handsome old fellow, as I remember him, and on Saturday, in Kendal, was always dressed in a tall silk hat and a green field-dress coat with brass buttons.

Before them again there were the Underbarrow Hounds, who stuck to the fox, and the names of some of their followers still remain: Richard Willison was master, and Brian Bell, Robert Dacre, and John Dickinson were often out with him.

I remember once meeting a scratch pack going home from hunting, and asking the huntsman what they hunted, he replied, "Hunt! They can hunt anything, from an elephant to a bumble-bee, and catch it too." Such were probably the hounds of this neighbourhood in the first half of the century.

In 1849 Walter Strickland, of Sizergh, started a pack of Harriers along with William Henry Wakefield, and for several seasons they hunted the country round Kendal, but about 1855 they separated and, though the Squire kept things going for another season, the pack was broken up in the following spring. I can just remember seeing these hounds hunting near Burneside.

In the year 1856, the country then being vacant, the late William Wilson, who had lately built his house at High Park, near Oxenholme, began to hunt the district, starting at first with some foot beagles which he had, and converting them as time went on into harriers. For the summer months they went out to walk with the surrounding farmers, and in the winter months were kennelled at Oxenholme. Old Tom Carradus, of Natland, was huntsman. Tom was a cheery old soul, and held firmly to the maxim that all time spent otherwise than hunting is wasted, and thought that "the pride of all pleasure is questing the hare," and a rare hand he was to quest, find, and kill her when he found. This pack was sold and went to the Isle of Wight in 1863.

Those who were keen hunters in the district felt that the country must be hunted somehow, and arrangements were made with Mr. Pearson, of Pool Bank, Crosthwaite, that his hounds should spend a week or two now and then in the Milnthorpe district. John Holme was the prime mover in the matter, and very well he rode on a wonderful brown cob which could get over anything. George Cartmel and his brother were always out. Edward Barton, too, who, I am glad to say, still rides right well, used to ride Toby, a great performer, Robert Hutton, the famous bonesetter, William Henry Wakefield, William Wilson, the late master, and a good many others, including, of course, Christopher Wilson, who was then at Cambridge, and William and Charles as lads. The pack was under the care of a mere lad, Dick Jackson, who has since become to this county the impersonation of hunting under the name of "Hunty Dick" – and whose cheery voice and view halloa have been to the Westmorland hares what John Peel's "Tally ho" was to the foxes of Cumberland. The hounds were put up at various farms and inns in the district, and the visit always ended with a dinner at the headquarters, when many a pleasant evening was spent discussing the week's sport.

In 1864 or 1865 Christopher Wilson, on leaving Cambridge, came home, and thinking that an occasional visit from Mr. Pearson's hounds was not enough, he purchased the hounds who had hunted the Ambleside district under his uncle, James Christopher Wilson, and began to hunt the country regularly with Jimmy Woodend carrying the horn. This went on for a year or two, but Jimmy was not so young as he was, and in 1870 Dick Jackson was induced to leave Crosthwaite and throw his fortune in with the Oxenholme pack, and since then, in varying forms, the hounds have been under his care, and long may he continue as kennel huntsman. A further improvement occurred in 1871, when Mr. Pearson gave up his hunt, and 15 couples of his harriers came to Oxenholme. From this date the present Oxenholme hunt begins its career; the Oxenholme Hunt button dates from then, and though the pack now exclusively hunt deer, the pedigrees of some of the existing pack could be traced back to the little cry of hounds which came from Crosthwaite.

With his improved pack, Christopher showed great sport, he rode hard and was a good huntsman, and when difficulties of scent or an intricate double were too great, Dick was always at hand to join in and help to set matters going again. Paddy and Hob-Goblin were his hunters in those days, and though after 30 years things loom big, yet I still believe that few finer jumpers ever existed than those two. For two years Fred Johnson, of Castlesteads, lived with Christopher at High Park, and those were amongst the best and merriest seasons the hounds had under his rule. The cares of agriculture and his stud farm soon began to take up his attention, and, though he was still master, Christopher was not always out, and about 1873 Charles Wilson was carrying the horn as often as not, though Christopher hunted them when he was there.

In the spring of 1878 Christopher announced his intention of giving up the hounds as acting master. A meeting of the hunt was held, and a committee was formed, and to that committee the hounds were made over with the condition that Charles Wilson was to be field master and that the country was to be hunted for five years as hitherto. New kennels had to be found, and the late William Henry Wakefield came to our rescue and offered to build on most reasonable terms. This offer the committee most gladly accepted, and in November 1878, the hounds moved to Endmoor with Dick Jackson as kennel huntsman. The change was an advantageous one in every way. William Henry Wakefield was our treasurer, and in this post he was succeeded by Jacob, his son, who now provides the second whip and helps the hunt with untiring energy in every way. Richard Gillow was our secretary, but volunteering took up so much of his time (he had become the colonel) that he gave up the secretaryship in 1879, and the present secretary, John Weston, took the office. He is a busy man, but notwithstanding all his other duties of business, volunteering, and county work, he has held the post ever since to the entire satisfaction of the hunt. He also assisted the hunt by whipping in, in a most efficient manner until the harriers were given up.

We had great sport, hares were plentiful, and all went well, and in 1886 the hunt testified their gratitude to the master and secretary by a present. We gave Charles Wilson a silver horn and John Weston a whip and a silver sandwich case as a small token of our esteem.

The memories of capital gallops we had are innumerable. Among the best was one from Low Levens to Crosthwaite and round by Dawson Fold to Brigsteer, where we killed. Another run stands out, when we found above Hincaster, and ran at a great pace by Whasset to Holme Park. The head of this hare still holds a position of honour in the master's house, being one of the stoutest of her race. One could go on with the accounts of stout hares and good runs till the reader was wearied of them.

In 1880 Richard Jackson was mounted for the first time, and he took to riding like a duck to water. I well remember how his whip got entangled in his horse's tail and his complete bewilderment as to where it was fast. "Whatever has got hold of my whip?" he shouted, while his horse plunged and kicked.

No account of the hunt would be complete without some allusion to the hunt dinner at Milnthorpe. For 20 years and more the wind-up of the season was the occasion of a dinner at the Cross Keys at Milnthorpe, given to the farmers whose land we crossed. About a hundred sat down, and a very convivial evening was spent with songs and the usual loyal and suitable toasts. Who can ever forget William Dobson's song about the "Old sow," " Boltons Yard," or "Nobbut a country Gaby?" "Hunty Dick" generally led off with his grand hare-hunting song, and late on in the evening, when the room was thick with tobacco smoke, he would sing "Old Towler" with "a hey, ho, cheery!" Surely "such harmony Handel himself never knew!" To us keen hunters the occasion was not unmixed with sadness as it was the wind-up of the season, and the summer had to be got through before we should again hear the horn and hound. In 1888 it was decided to give up the dinner and try a new venture with a ball at Kendal, so that many more, including our younger friends, the brave lads and fair lasses of Westmorland, could join in the fun. These balls were a great success.

On February 8th, 1888, a completely new departure was made, when a red deer was enlarged at Low Bleaze, and stag-hunting was begun. Hares had become scarce, and it was no use spending whole days looking for fur. From 1888 to 1894 we hunted hare and stag on alternate days, but in November, 1894, we bade farewell to the Oxenholme harriers and livery of green, and the Oxenholme stag hounds, with scarlet livery began their career. A change also was made in the hounds; it was found that no horseman could live with the speedy harriers across our intricate and hilly Westmorland country, and the black and tan bloodhound cross was introduced. Opinions may differ as to the value of the bloodhound cross, for the hounds thus bred are sometimes delicate, in spite of Dick Jackson's devoted care in the kennel, and they suffer from cold and wet. They hang somewhat on the line, and do not score to cry as freely as foxhounds or harriers, but they hunt with untiring energy and persistence; they have grand voices and, above all, they run slower, so that we now have a chance to see many a good hunt which with faster hounds would be a stern chase from find to finish.

The herd of deer are kept in the roomy paddocks above Oxenholme. We began with half a dozen, but there are now more than 20 in the paddock, besides a considerable number of deer at large in various parts of the country. At first we hunted stags and hinds, but of late the herd has consisted almost entirely of haviers, as the hinds are more apt to be hurt, and stags are sometimes sulky and will not run. As often as not we draw for a deer which has been harboured, and though the carted deer often gives capital sport still there is an added spice of enjoyment when the run comes after the uncertainty of a draw which is sometimes long and tedious.

Stag hunting is sometimes said to be a cruel sport. This is entirely untrue so far as the Oxenholme Hunt is concerned. No doubt a tired deer is a melancholy object, but so is a tired fox or a tired hare. The deer are hardly ever touched by the hounds, but they like their liberty and do not like being touched or handled, and sometimes they hurt themselves when they are caught. All sport is more or less coupled with pain, but there is certainly less pain to the quarry in stag-hunting than in any other line of sport which the heart of man has devised as yet.

Of the sport Charles Wilson has shown since 1894 whole books might be written. And I cannot help mentioning a few of the days which have become almost historical. Memory is a store-house in which it is a pleasure to rummage, and though the actual sport of to-day, with its hopes and fears of what the sport will be, of how one's horse will go, or how the weather will turn out, is the important thing in hunting, still the bare outline of some of the runs that have taken place during the last dozen years are worth recording.

Mabel was the first great deer. She ran for seven seasons with never a scratch, and at last the master felt she had earned her rest, and sent her back to Gowbarrow Fell, whence she came. Since when she has bred several hinds, and for ought I know is still wondering when she will again be caught and turned out for a chase.

Lion, was and is another great deer. In the spring of 1897 he discovered a brilliant line between Dallam Tower Park and the Covers at Endmoor, and ran back and forward several times, and never was caught till, on the last day of the season, he jumped into Levens Park, where he was left to spend the summer. Since then he has been caught several times, and turned out in different parts of the country. He has more than once gone to the Lune, but wherever he starts from he, more often than not, looks round for Levens Park, and ends his run safe within its hospitable walls.

November 25th, 1892, saw us at Greenhead, and on hounds being laid on, they crossed the canal and made for Preston Hall. We had a climb to the Warth, and from thence to Lupton Tarn, and up to Barkin House. Thence to Holmescales, Barrows Green, and up the valley to Shaw End, where hounds were called off. About 18 miles in all. December 29th, 1893, was a great day. The meet was at Burton, and so dense was the fog that the master was in doubts as to the safety of turning out, but as there was a slight clearing the deer was enlarged, and was not taken till within a mile or two of Bay Horse, in the country over which Mr. Ormrod now shows such excellent sport. The Lune was crossed near Halton.

On December 29th, 1896, a wonderful hunt took place. The meet was at Hundhow, for a deer which had been harboured in the Side House Woods. He crossed the Kent at once and, leaving Staveley on the right, crossed the hills to Windermere. He swam the lake above Bowness, while the hounds were taken round by the Ferry. They hit off the line on the far side, and continued the hunt through the hanging woods above the lake, and over the brow to Esthwaite. There he was seen, and a boat was procured and the deer captured as he was coming out on the Grizedale side. A penn'orth of all sorts with a vengeance!

On April 1st, 1808, Lion was known to be in the covers at Grimeshill. Finding himself disturbed he started north, after a preliminary ring, and followed the valley nearly to Lowgill. Then he turned and coming back through Firbank, kept his face southwards by Killington Reservoir, Black Esset, and finally was taken in the farm buildings at Overthwaite. A very remarkable hunt!

March 3rd, 1800, was about as cold and windy a morning as I remember, and it seemed a long way to go to Aughton for a somewhat doubtful outlier. However we went, and though we were fairly chilled to the bone when the deer went away, the run which followed more than made amends. Crossing the Lune at once we ran at best pace to Hornby and, turning left-handed across the Wenning, again crossed Lune below Gressingham. The deer led us over a very fine line to Arkholme, and thence turned west as far as Docker Park, and crossing the Midland Railway took us up on to Whittington Fell, and once more sinking the hill was finally taken in the Lune near Thurland Castle. A very fine run over a most glorious country!

As a contrast to this last run, a deer was known to be somewhere near Lowgill, and a meet was fixed on April 13th, 1800, at Cold Seat. Not an inviting title. The deer was found, and led the hunt up the valley to Tebay, and on to Gaisgill and Kelleth. Here he turned up to the Fells and dropped down into the Langdale valley, and was finally taken in the very heart of the hills in the wildest and remotest spot imaginable, some 25 miles from the kennels.

On March 8th, 1901, we met at Burrow for an outlier. The deer was soon found in a cover hard by, and took us over some of the finest grass country to Black Burton and on by Bentham to Wennington, and was finally taken near Upper Bentham after a hunt of about two hours and a half. The first part of which was simply glorious!

Middleton Hall was the fixture for March 16th, 1901, for a hind who was known to be on Barbon Fell. After a turn round the fell she sank to the valley. Crossed Lune near Rigmaden, and finally was left at peace in Levens Park. About as unlikely a meet as possible for sport, followed by as fine a hunt as this country can give.

This season has already left its memorable days on the calendar. A deer enlarged at Greenhead has been taken at Shaw End; a 14 mile point. Another found near Cockrigg led the hunt over Benson Knott, by Moresdale Hall, past Killington Reservoir to Killington Woods. In Lowther Wood a hind was found, who led us past Whittington Woods to Arkholme, and thence by Thurland Castle to Black Burton, and finally ran us out of scent near Kirkby Lonsdale Station. A beautiful hunt over a grand country!

These thread-bare accounts might be amplified to any extent, and only tell of a very few of the memorable days there have been. Deer have been taken at Littledale, Moiling, Dent, Kentmere, Gummershow, and at many other places far away outside of our old hunting boundaries. A larger establishment is needed; our master still carries the horn with untiring devotion and has become a past master of the wood craft needful to unravel every dodge of a tricky deer, and when the quarry is at bay he can throw a lasso about as well as any living Englishman. He has the assistance of two energetic hard-riding whips, who are always at hand when the pack are to be stopped or turned or brought together. For our first whip, William Hully, there can be nothing but unstinted praise, no country can stop him, and he seems to have an almost magical knack of being where he is wanted and his pluck and determination in handling and housing a violent deer are unrivalled.

Our country is by no means all plain sailing, you cannot take it as it comes in many parts of it, and it requires both knowledge and memory of possibilities to live with hounds especially on the higher fell ground. It is the variety of the country we cross in which lies the charm. What greater pleasure can there be than, after toiling over a range of fell, to see hounds sinking the hill and to know that a stretch of sound grass and negotiable fences lie before us? The scenery, too, in an endless delight; each day brings its own different effects of light and colour, and the Lake mountains, Morecambe Bay, and the valleys of the Kent and Lune are a continual joy to behold.

No hunt can get on without the support of the farmers, and those who farm the land we ride over are good farmers, the best of good fellows, and, above all, most kindly disposed to the hunt. I can hardly remember a cross word being spoken in 30 years. Still there is no doubt that wire is a cheap and quick way of mending a fence, or stopping a gap we may have made, and farming is not the easy job it was 30 years ago. There has been and there is wire in the country, especially in some districts, and for a few years after its invention it spread apace, but now we are liberal with rails, and hope the worst is past. The farmers too begin to find that barbed wire is nasty prickly stuff, and when the posts rot and it gets trailing about it may easily injure the stock, and even in the fences it is unsightly and may be dangerous.

Long may the Hunt prosper under its present admirable management.

C. J. C., December, 1902.

The Lunesdale & Oxenholme Staghounds
by William Scarth-Dixon

The Staghound Country

The Oxenholme country is in the county of Westmorland and is some fifty miles long by twenty miles wide, and consists chiefly of grass and moorland, with a good deal of wood. The country chiefly associated with the chase of the wild red deer, extends from Wharton Crag, near Carnforth, to Grange-over-Sands on Morecambe Bay, and then by Cartmel Fell to Windermere Lake, which is the north-western boundary. Thence it returns in a northeasterly direction as far as Tebay in Yorkshire, and thence due south by way of Sedbergh to Kirkby Lonsdale. It is a good scenting country, wild in many places, but a country with which high-class sport is closely associated. As for the horse to ride, the wise man who is casting in his lot with such a pack will ride the horse of the country. He will be the best and the safest.

The best centres are perhaps Kendal and Milnthorpe.

History

The history of the Oxenholme Staghounds is a very interesting one and as has been the case with many first-rate packs of hounds which have become famous in history, it had somewhat humble origin. Some sixty-seven years ago, Mr. William Wilson, of High Park, Oxenholme, established a pack of foot beagles which he subsequently converted to harriers. In 1863 the harrier were sold, and Mr. Pearson, of Crosthwaite, hunted the country by invitation.

In 1864 or 1865, Mr. Christopher Wilson, of Rigmaden, purchased his uncle's pack, which had hunted the Ambleside district and took over the Mastership, and for some years Mr. Pearson and he seem to have hunted the Oxenholme country between them. In 1871, Mr. Pearson gave up, and Mr. Wilson added his hounds and country to the Oxenholme.

Mr. Christopher Wilson retired in 1878, and then succeeded the long Mastership of Mr. Charles H. Wilson, which lasted some forty-five years. In a way, Mr. Charles H. Wilson may be said to have made the country, for the many changes it underwent practically all took place in his Mastership.

A shortening supply of hares in the country brought matters to a climax in the later eighties and in 1888 the first red deer was enlarged, and until 1894, hare and stag were hunted on alternate days. In 1894 stag became the sole quarry.

Hunting the red deer in such a country presented many problems not very easy of solution, but Mr Wilson was the man to solve them. Outlying deer soon became plentiful, for it is sufficiently obvious that it was impossible to keep on terms with hounds that could run down a perfectly fit stag in a couple of hours, or less in such a country. So gradually the number of outlying deer increased. Then there were a few wild deer in, the country. The Hasells, of Dalemain, have, it is said, hunted the wild red deer of Martindale Forest from time immemorial, and from Martindale Forest deer kept straying, till now the Lunesdale and Oxenholme may be said to hold a corresponding place in Westmorland to what the Devon and Somerset do in Somersetshire.

A word about the breeding of the Oxenholme Stag hounds may be of interest. In Mr. Christopher Wilson's day, and for some time after, the Oxenholme Staghounds were a cross between the old Southern Harrier (the blue mottled harrier) and the rough Welsh foxhound, crossed again with the bloodhound by Mr. Charles Wilson. They were big powerful hounds, but slow. They were, however, admirably adapted for the country; had great perseverance and a wonderful "cry." When Mr. Heaton took hold of the country, all these hounds had been sold, and at first he hunted the red deer with the Vale of Lune Harriers, hunting hare and deer alternately. However, he soon tired of this and set to work to breed a new pack of hounds with the harriers as a foundation. These he crossed with Foxhounds, Cotley Harriers, Scarteen Black and Tan, Rough Welsh, and Blue Mottled Harriers, and he also got back some of Mr. Charles Wilson's old blood. The result is two packs of wonderful hounds, close hunters and persevering, with which he hunts the wild deer and the hare.

Mr. Wilson retired in 1918, after a Mastership of forty-five years. He was succeeded by Mr. J. R. Heaton, of Melling Hall, near Carnforth. The Hon. Secretary is Mr. J. W. Cropper, Summerhow, Kendal, and the Hon. Treasurer is Mr. B. H. Satterthwaite, Castle Park, Lancaster. The kennels are at Gatebeck, Endmoor, Kendal, and Charles Turner is the kennel huntsman and first whipper-in.

Mr. Jacob Wakefield is now Field Master and Mr. C. Hulme Wilson is Deputy Master of the Staghounds.

Short biographies of some of the well known people mentioned.

William Henry Wakefield was not only a most important and influential person in Kendal, he was also very well known around the district as an excellent horseman and huntsman. He built a family house at Sizergh where he lived along with a farm of 500 acres. He took an active interest in town affairs, was a town councillor, and was twice the Mayor. He was Chairman of the Farmers Club, senior partner in the Kendal Bank, a senior magistrate of Westmorland and Chairman of the Quarter Sessions. He was High Sheriff of Westmorland in 1871 and Deputy Lieutenant of the County.

William Henry Wakefield.

The Cropper Family of Burneside

Hunting was an obsession with Charles J. Cropper. It is likely that it is he who is mentioned in reports of the exploits of the Oxenholme Staghounds. He hunted with 75 packs in his lifetime. During 1900-1910, when hunting on horse was periodically banned during the period of official mourning for the late Queen Victoria, he spent 35 days hunting on foot. He chose to hunt foxes rather than work on making profit for the family firm. (Burneside Paper Mill). Between 1880 and 1914 he spent over 1,340 days away hunting in packs nationwide – an average of almost 40 days per season, usually at weekends. His most popular day for hunting was Friday. He produced a book, *Hunting Scraps*, which contained hundreds of drawings and watercolours drawn and painted by him during his 47 years hunting with friends and family. Although frequently away hunting he did not entirely neglect the family firm. He was wholeheartedly dedicated to paper making. A painting of him by George Armour exists which shows him in hunting attire seated on his horse, "Commando". He resigned as a full-time director in 1907 but by June 1914 he was back managing the mills. In his final years he hunted for 36 days despite suffering from gout. On 6 October 1924 he died after an accident on the hunting field, aged 72.

James Winstanley Cropper was sent to a preparatory school in Berkshire in 1891 from where he went to Eton and Cambridge. After graduation he spent a year at the accountants, Price Waterhouse, in London. In August 1900 at his 21st birthday party, he announced his intention to assist in the management of the family run paper mill. 1902 he began work with James Cropper & Co. In February 1903 he went on an eight-month journey through Europe, the Far East, Canada and New York. Whether this was merely for pleasure or in connection with his work is unclear. From 1907 to 1914 he hunted as often as two days a week in the winter months. Much of the year was spent in shooting to flush out the game on the estate, often in the company of young apprentices from the mills. His enthusiasm for field sports meant that he was absent from the mills for weeks at a time. While hunting in North Yorkshire he was kicked on the head by a horse and spent a month in a hospital in Darlington recuperating from an operation on his skull. In June that year he spent a month on a tour of Canada and Japan with his wife – perhaps recovering from the accident. He was later the Honorary Secretary of the Oxenholme Staghounds. James's only son, Anthony was born in 1912 and was also a keen member of the hunt. His wife, Philippa, is still alive today, although elderly, and clearly remembers riding with the hounds.

The Heaton family were another prominent family at that time and lived at a large house at Prizet, just south of Kendal. All the family rode the hounds and as previously mentioned, Mr John Heaton became Master in 1918. The last remaining member mentioned in the narrative is Martin Heaton who now lives in Scotland, the family having left the area many years ago.

Miss Somervell, also mentioned in the text, was one of the Somervell family who owned the local shoe factory (Somervell Brothers Ltd.) which was better known as K. Shoes.

Mr J. R. Heaton.

Extracts From the *Westmorland Gazette*

11th February 1888

There was a large turnout of sportsmen yesterday in Old Hutton to participate in a stag hunt – an unusual occurrence in this part of the country. The scene was a most picturesque one, for besides there being over 200 spectators there were carriages, and nearly half a hundred of mounted sportsmen. It is seldom such a sight is witnessed in South Westmorland. One of the best riders was a little fellow of about eight years, on a grey pony, and attired in proper hunting costume. A Kendal publican essayed a spin with the hounds, but the first fence proved fatal to his seat. The hunt was a most enjoyable one throughout.

ACCIDENT TO A HARRIER. – On Monday an accident happened to a valuable hound belonging to the Oxenholme Harriers. The unfortunate animal had just stepped upon the railway north of Elmsfield, Milnthorpe, when it was caught by a light engine from Preston to Windermere and one of its forelegs cut off, besides being badly injured internally. The driver of the engine did his best to avoid the accident, but it was too late. Mr Helm, foreman platelayer, coming up at the time, at once put the poor animal out of' its misery. The loss of this hound is regretted, as it had taken one or more prizes.

*A STAG HUNT NEAR KENDAL (**From a Correspondent**)*
On Thursday the Oxenholme Harriers met at Low Bleaze to try hunting the deer. The morning was delightful as good air and bright sunshine could make it, and a goodly number turned out on horse, foot and wheels to see the deer uncarted. At 11.15 the van doors were opened and away went the deer, a fine red hind, in the direction of Birkrigg Park, making little of the walls and fences that lay in the way. In a few minutes the hounds were laid on and went away at score. Near Birkrigg Park, the deer waited and the pack came up to her, but she popped over the high gate into a lane, and from there she led us as hard as legs could carry us, by Summerlands and Stainton to Sellet Hall, where she took to the canal. The hounds were called off, and away she went again by Viver and Greenhead to Milton, and there she was taken and sent home. The point of the run was about six miles, much more as we went, and every one went home well pleased with the first trial at a deer hunt with the Oxenholme Harriers.

. . . .

We have also obtained the following report of the run:-
Lovers of the chase in the neighbourhood of Kendal had a memorable hunt on Thursday, when a stag was liberated and afforded some exciting sport. Many of the older inhabitants will remember a stag hunt should have taken place in the country about Helm 40 years ago, but on being carted to the place it was found, to the great disappointment of a large "field", that the animal had been suffocated on its journey to the trysting place. Again, a few years later, another stag was hunted, and provided a lively chase towards Ackenthwaite, where the animal held the hounds gamely at bay. Since then none of the larger game have been hunted in the southern part of Westmorland, and when it was whispered that the Oxenholme Hunt Committee had procured some stags everyone was on tip-toe of excitement to know when one was to be liberated and where the meet would take place. During the present season the Oxenholme Harriers

have provided some fine sport. The hounds, in fact, are as much at home when giving Reynard a brisk spin, as when they are following the hare. It is unfortunate that the latter game is becoming exceedingly scarce, and considerable preservation has to be resorted to both by farmers – who always enjoy a run with the hounds and welcome the harriers on their land - and the committee of the Hunt. The fixture on Thursday was at Low Bleaze, a trimly kept farm in Old Hutton occupied by Messrs. Procter and Sons. The fact of a stag having to be run on this occasion soon leaked out, and on the evening previous the prospect of the run was a matter of public comment. The animals – three red hinds – had been obtained from Lowther Park. The morning was a beautiful one, being more like an April morn than one in February "fill-dyke". It was a morning in which all could join in the well known hunting rhyme:-

We'll all go a-hunting today,
All nature looks smiling and gay;
So we'll join the glad throng
That goes laughing along,
And we'll all go a-hunting today.

The meet was at 11 o'clock in the forenoon, and long before this hour numbers of spectators had proceeded along the road in the direction of Bleaze Hall. At the hour appointed the site was an exceedingly charming one, as there would be nearly 250 on "shank's pony", while there were several carriages, and over 40 ladies and gentlemen mounted. The latter included Mr. C.H. Wilson (Master), Mr. J.W. Weston (Whip), Mr. W.C. Strickland, Miss Strickland, Sizergh Castle; Mr. C.J. Cropper, Mr. Jacob Wakefield, Dr. Illiffe, Mr. Barton, the Misses Barton (4), Mr. & Mrs. Proctor, Curwen Woods, Miss Lonsdale, Carlisle; Mr. Crane, Mr. Backhouse, Mr. Hunt, Lancaster; Misses Hunt, Master Hunt, Mr. Pugh, Ingmire; Mr. J. Logan, Lowwood, Mr. Rigg, Appleby; Mr. J. Rigg, Windermere; Mr. T. Rigg, Grange, etc.

The stag was taken to Bleaze Hall in a covered cart, the place where it was liberated being the rising ground behind the farmhouse. It was decided to give the animal ten minutes start. The stag was let out of the cart with the crack of numerous whips, the desire of the huntsmen being to turn its head in the direction of Holmescales. In this, however, they were disappointed, for on reaching the dip of the field the course was not sufficiently guarded, and instead of taking the course to Holmescales the stag bolted off towards Gatebeck. Away it bounded across country, negotiating every obstacle it encountered with the greatest ease, and the followers – both horse and foot – were in the highest glee at the prospect of a grand run. The hounds were almost wild with the strong scent, and went at a rattling pace. When near Gatebeck the stag took to the high road, which it kept for a considerable distance from the village, and then it took down Stainton lane – where it was encountered by a pedestrian – and into the open again on the Millbridge ground at the back of Summerlands. The hounds managed to get close up, so close indeed on the land on the Sellett Hall Estate, at the bottom end of Stainton, that the stag took to the canal. The hounds leapt into the water after it, but in a short time several horsemen were up and the hounds were whipped off. The game was a little loathe to leave the water; yet, 20 minutes afterwards, it put its foot on terra firma and galloped off. It was again decided to allow the stag a few minutes grace before the hounds were let loose, and on the signal for a start being given a merry chorus was heard. The stag had taken across country in the direction of Farleton Knot; after a sharp run the hounds overtook their game, and, after a bit of fencing, the stag jumped into a hedge to get away from its enemy. Here the huntsmen came upon the scene, the hounds were whipped off, and the stag liberated from its position and carted home. The hunt was an excellent one, and another run is anticipated.

15th December 1888

Stag Hunts Near Kendal – Some fine runs have recently been enjoyed by members of the Oxenholme Hunt, in consequence of the new arrangement by which a stag is hunted each week. Many persons – a correspondent writes – talk about the cruelty practised in hunting the deer, but to anyone who has witnessed a hunt there is nothing to hurt the most sensitive feelings of anyone. The greatest precautions are taken by the Hunt Committee to prevent cruelty, and, in fact the deer is very well able, owing to its fleetness, to look after itself. On Friday the meet was at Whassett, near Milnthorpe, when the day was fine and there was a good muster of horsemen. After the stag was slipped from the cart it went off in the direction of Overthwaite, fences and every obstacle being negotiated with the greatest of ease and coolness. Taking right across country, it led through Farleton to near Cow Brow, when the quarry turned in the direction of Newbiggin Fell, going between Farleton Crag and Hutton Roof. She next paid a visit to Holme, and after dodging about for some time, at last took refuge in the peat-house of Mr Coulthwaite, of the Commercial Hotel, the hounds being in close attendance. The distance covered was slightly over a dozen miles. When the stag was making towards the village of Holme it was evidently regarded as a great curiosity. A farmer followed the animal at break neck pace down a lane adjoining his land, and averred that he could have caught it had he only been able to retain his breathing powers. A six-barred gate, however, was placed between him and the deer, the result of a jump from the latter. On the stag being captured, the huntsman were soon up, and a crowd collected to witness the unusual sight. A fine specimen of the red buck had been obtained from Gowbarrow, and it was determined to give him a run on Tuesday. The meet was at Oxenholme at eleven o'clock. Owing to the frost in the ground the start was postponed for an hour, when there was a large assemblage of both horsemen and pedestrians. The stag was taken to a field near the Punch Bowl Inn, and on being liberated he bounded off towards Helm, taking its entire length on the Natland side to near the Station Inn. He returned on the Stainton side of the Helm, and those who had taken a position on the knot were afforded a splendid view. The stag went close to the field from whence he started, and taking some stiff fences and going over the hill, came to St Sunday's Beck. After some time running the stag was retaken and conveyed home.

From the **Westmorland Gazette Nov. 9, 1889**
WILLIAM HENRY WAKEFIELD
ANNOUNCEMENT OF DEATH.

We have to announce with the deepest regret the awfully sudden death of Mr. W. H. Wakefield, of Sedgwick, which occurred on Friday, the 8th inst, about three o'clock Mr. Wakefield had been hunting with the Oxenholme Harriers, and was apparently in the best of health. After hunting some time, the master, Mr. Charles Wilson, was about to call the dogs off and return to the kennels, when Mr. Wakefield asked that the hounds should be tried again as he was enjoying the sport so much. A hare was found and was run into upon Mr. Wakefield's farm at Wellheads. Mr. Wakefield rode well up to the hounds and leapt off his horse and secured the hare. He held the hare up, and almost immediately fell dead. The sad news has created a feeling of profound sorrow and sympathy for the family of the deceased. Mr. Wakefield was the only son of the late Mr. John Wakefield, of Sedgwick, and was 61 years of age. A messenger was immediately despatched to Kendal for Dr. Noble, who at once proceeded to Sedgwick. On an examination of the body he pronounced death to have been the result of heart disease. Eight or nine years ago Mr. Wakefield was the subject of heart disease, and he was warned against hunting or other violent exercises. Greatly improved health appears to have influenced Mr. Wakefield in relaxing these restrictions, for he frequently of late indulged in hunting and driving. Mr. Wakefield's nephew, Mr. J. W. Weston, who was in the hunting field, and close up to Mr. Wakefield, hurried to his assistance, and he died in his nephew's arms.

His last moments as recorded by James Cropper. "He sprang from his horse to get the hare and the next moment fell back helpless. His nephew, Mr Weston was a few yards behind him and was at once at his side but with another breath he expired".

30th December 1893

HUNTING A LOST DEER. - *On Tuesday at Arnside, there was a large influx of mounted ladies and gentlemen in hunting costume and a considerable number of pedestrians all bent on having an enjoyable run with the hounds, in search of the deer, which was lost some three weeks ago near Silverdale, and which had since been seen on several occasions in the neighbourhood of the Knott and Arnside park. It was intended to endeavour to drive the deer in the direction of the shore when the tide was in, to induce it to take to the water and so capture it with boats, it having previously been across the channel to Meathop, but when found by the dogs in Arnside park the deer took the opposite direction, and went along the marsh to the Cave, through Silverdale, and regaining the marsh near the pumping engine for draining Leighton mosses, it took across towards the Slag Bank, and was lost to view.*

5th January 1901

THE OXENHOLME STAGHOUNDS – *Mr. C. H. Wilson, the master, was met on Thursday last week by Lady Henry Bentinck, Lady Alice Egerton, Miss Jenkinson, the Misses Barton, Mrs Crane, Miss Cropper, the Misses Cheetham, Lord Henry Bentinck, Messrs Jacob Wakefield, C. J. Cropper, J. W. Weston, E. Sharpe, J. Rigg, W. F. Egerton, R. Rigg, E. C. Backhouse, G. W. Brumwell, J. P. Atkinson, J. C. Carden, A. W. Wingate-Saul, Bruce Rigg, J. Cropper, M. Radcliffe and others. The rallying point was at Lupton Smithy, where at noon a deer was enlarged and provided a clinking hunt of close upon three hours duration. – On Monday there was a large meet at Barrows Green, the field including Lady Alice Egerton, Miss Barton, Mrs Crane, Miss Ormerod, Miss Jenkinson, the Misses Cheetham, Miss Cropper and Messrs C. W. Wilson, W. F. Egerton, A. W. Wingate-Saul, J. W. Weston, J. C. Carden, J. P. Atkinson, R. Bowness, E. C. Backhouse, Mr. Radcliffe, W. Bruce Logan, J. Logan, G. W. and Master Brumwell, E. Barton, R. Rigg, Bruce Rigg, C. Cropper, J. Cropper, Jacob Wakefield, and others. Messrs Hully, Jackson and Barber acted as whips. It was a delightful morning, a perfect hunting day, and fully one hundred people from Kendal and the neighbourhood were assembled on Helm. An outlying stag had been viewed the previous day on the very summit of the fell, and today he was discovered harboured in Castlestead Wood. Hounds soon had him afoot, but he seemed loath to leave the vicinity. At last he broke away on the western side, hurried over Helm Pastures, crossed the highroad at Sinkfalls, ran parallel with the London* and North Western Railway to Moorhouse Farm, where the hounds were stopped to allow the large scattered field to get together. Hounds now swept off towards Crosscrake Church, forward to Hincaster and Woodhouse. The stag went on to Heversham Head, right through the Covers, out by Eversley, and over the road near the old toll-bar at the corner of the garden belonging to Levens Hall. Nimbly he pegged away by Ninezergh Farm, dashed through the Kent, and forged along by Low Levens Bottoms. The hunt now became fast and exciting. At High Foulshaw for some minutes he was lost to sight. Meeting young Jack Brennan, the master enquired in what direction he had gone, but he answered that he had not seen him. At Ulpha Marsh, his father, portly old Jack, keeper to Mr. Bromley Wilson, came to the rescue. Hat in hand, and his entire heart in the sport, he indicated the direction the deer had taken, and as the master galloped past him, he shouted, "the Missis has gone to watch where stag comes out of the channel, and will put you right." Few things transpire in Ulpha, which escape the sharp eye of genial old Jack Brennan! Through the big covers behind Jack's cottage on the sea shore swept our vigorous quarry, but hounds were enabled to hit the line again. The quarry had left the sea, and both they and the field were in close proximity. Over the bank he cunningly hid himself in a bed of willows, but his remorseless enemies drove him out over Grange Marsh at a rattling pace. Near the Gas Works at Grange he crossed the Furness Railway line, and tearing across the sands, plunged into the sea, followed by the pack. The master and the whips had an arduous task to get the hounds back, as they had become almost invisible in the far off water. Where the stag went no one knows, but when he discovered that he was no longer being chased, he would probably come to shore about Silverdale. He had finished an exhilarating chase of three hours. E. B.

23rd September 1905
OXENHOLME STAG HOUNDS – The above pack had a most enjoyable and useful run for the young entry at Arnside on Saturday after outlying deer. The Cragg Wood and Arnside Knott having been drawn blank, hounds were put into Middlebarrow Wood and at once the old hounds began to scatter and speak to the line of deer, which proved correct, as two big deer were seen to be stealing through the covert in front of hounds. Dick Jackson's "Tally Ho" soon made it evident to all that they had broken covert at the Silverdale side. Hounds were soon out and on the line, making all resound with music. On they went as if for Eves Wood, when our deer was seen to be heading back over Silverdale Common with the pack in close attendance. They drove him through Far Arnside Woods into Moleholes Gill, down the gill into Arnside Park, across the park to Blackstour Point, and being so hard pressed he took to the sea and was eventually taken after a hard bit of rowing by the boatman, who had been waiting patiently for him for some time. He was brought to shore and comfortably housed at New Barns in a loose box and on Monday removed to the paddocks at Oxenholme. The hunt was enjoyed by many, some on horseback and some on foot.

22nd December 1934 (see mention in narrative)
OXENHOLME STAG HOUNDS – These hounds met at Old Town last Thursday andwere taken to Mansergh Big Wood to draw. There were signs of deer about but none could be found, and after drawing through Underley Gardens and Terry Bank Wood without finding, hounds were taken to Stony Park. Four hinds were found lying out here and ran down to the river, back up the heights and over Rigmaden Moor, and down again to the river at Holme House. They kept on downstream to below Underley, where they turned and ran up

again to Fleshbeck, where hounds were stopped after a pleasant river hunt. On Monday the meet was at Gilpin Bridge. Hounds were taken to draw the Witherslack Woods and found a hind on the outcast. She ran back into the woods and roe deer spoiled the chance of a hunt. A stag had been seen away towards Halecote, so hounds were gathered and taken on. He ran on to the Halecote Moss, where he put up two hinds which hounds then hunted across to Ulpha, and were stopped on the shores of the estuary.

List of members mentioned in this narrative

Ashworth, Capt.

Barlow Mr.

Benson (possibly Bunson), Colonel

Bentley, Mr.

Bentley, Miss

Bickersteth (possibly Bickarsteth), Miss
    (Lived at Casterton)

Brook, Mrs.

Buna? (poss Burra), Miss
    (Lived at Sedbergh)

Clark, Miss

Crewdson, Colonel

Crewdson, Miss Deborah

Cresswell, Mr.

Cropper. Mr. Anthony
    (Lived at Burneside)

Cropper, Major   "

Cropper, Miss Nancy "

Darlington, Miss

Dickinson, Mr. George
    (Lived at Cark-in-Cartmel)

Dickinson, Mr. Peter "

Dickinson, Mr. Tony "

Dobson, Mr. Harry (Lived at Sampool)

Dobson, Mr. Alan (Lived at Sampool)

Drew, Miss Hermione
    (Lived at Leasgill, Heversham)

Drew, Miss D   "

Drew, Miss W   "

Gadd, Mr.

Gardner, Mr. Harold

Harrison Broadley, Mr.

Heaton, Mr. Dick (Lived at Prizet)

Heaton, Mr. John (Lived at Prizet)

Heaton, Mr. Martin (Lived at Prizet)

Heaton, Miss Mary (Lived at Prizet)

Hodgson, Mr. Sam

Hodgson, Miss Margaret

Hook, Mrs.

Johnson, Mr.

King, Mr.

King, Mrs.

Lee, Mr. Harold

Lees, Miss (plus groom) (Windermere)

Locke-King, Mr. (Lived at Singleton Park)

North, Mr. Alan

North, Colonel Oliver (Lived at Lilymere)

North, Colonel Piers

Prior-Palmer, Capt. E.R.

Radcliffe, Miss Reynolds,

Reynolds, Mr. James (Lived at Leighton Hall)

Reynolds, Mrs.   "

Reynolds, Miss Daphne   "

Rigg, Mr. Bruce (Lived at Windermere)

Rigg, Mrs. Morden   "

Rigg, Miss Mary   "

Robinson, Mr.

Rutter, Mr. Jimmy (King's Arms, Kendal)

Rutter, Miss   "

Scott, Mr. Philip (Lived at Windermere)

Sherritt?

Smith, Mr.

Smith, Miss

Somervell, Miss

Stanley, Mr. Michael (Lived at Witherslack)

Stanley, Miss   "

Stuart-Richardson, Sir Ian Rory Hay

Todd, Mr.

Weston, Miss (Master of the Hounds)

While, Miss Diana (Lived at Haverthwaite)

Willink, Mr. Chris (Lived at Endmoor)

Willink, Mr. Peter (Lived at Endmoor)

Wilson, Mr. Edward (Teddy) (Lived at Rigmaden)

Wilson, Mr. Eric (Lived at Rigmaden)

Wilson, Mrs. (Lived at Rigmaden)

Miss Weston, Master of the Hunt, 1934

Miss Weston (left) and Miss Wakefield (right)

Mr J. R. Heaton on White
Wine at Ingleton, 1921.
Master of the Oxenholme
Hunt from 1918

Mr J. R. Heaton (centre),
Master of the Oxenholme
Hunt from 1918

Miss G. Smith, Mr W.
Wakefield and Miss D.
Garnett (Dallam 1928)

Mr J. Cropper (Treasurer) and Mrs J. R. Heaton

Mr G. Dickinson, Mrs Russel and Miss R. Reynolds

Mr Turner, Mr J. R. Heaton, Mr C. Wilson, Mrs Shepherd and Mr R. Clapham (Brigsteer)

Mr J. R. Heaton, H. Dobson and Mr. Crewdson meet at the Derby Arms

Anthony Cropper (Top Hat) and Mr. James Cropper (right)

This page and overleaf:
Hunt at Dallam Tower, 1928

Above: The Hunt takes to the Sands (Morecambe Bay)

Right: Wild Stag taken by the Lunesdale and Oxenholme Staghounds in Lake Windermere

Vale of Lune Harriers at Melling Hall, Mr J. R. Heaton Master

Meet of the Staghounds at Dallam Towers, Milnthorpe

Nature Note Book

There is only one cure for all maladies sure
Which reaches the heart to the core,
'Tis to follow the horn, on a fine hunting morn,
And where is the heart wishing more?
It turneth the grave into gay,
Makes pain unto pleasure give way,
Makes the weak become strong,
And the old become young,
So we'll all go a hunting today.

DEDICATED TO THE LESSER MONSTER.

THE

OXENHOLME HOUNDS

WHEN, WHERE, AND HOW THEY HUNTED

SEASON 1934-5

AND ALSO TO WHAT EXTENT MAN
WAS ABLE TO LIVE WITH THEM, ALL
THIS SET DOWN DIRECT FROM PERSONAL
OBSERVATIONS AND UNDERSTANDINGS·
BY THE FAT DREW OTHERWISE KNOWN
AS HARRIET, HALCYONE, ALMARNY OR HAG.

In the above group, reading from left to right, back
row :– Warrior, Denmark, Woodbine, Watchful, Liberty, Mr Dinnerbell,
behind: Lofty, Wagtail and Hermit. Front row :– Mr Warrington, Lightning,
Cooter, Sparkler, Novice, Mr Duster, Dame Daisy, Lord Craftsman,
little Mermaid, Wellington, Mr Daniel, Leighton, Lincoln and Network'

Oct: 18th

Miss Weston on her new horse LIONEL.

Miss Drew shows Handsome Hounds.

Miss Crewdson engages Tanking gear out of the seeds.

Picture of monster spying on hounds in distress. Deer escaping.

Oct: 26th

Miss Weston decides it is a wet day.

Hounds running up and over Whitbarrow.

The owners of newly purchased young horses are very careful not to overdo them

OCTOBER 18th THURSDAY.

Hounds met at the AA. Box at Carnforth Level. The silly little Yealand deer with shredded ears was found in a field behind Hyning. It ran through the park and across towards Yealand, but doubled back to the park. It ran out again and turned down towards the road, just north of Skees Bridge, and disappeared. By this time the hounds had had enough and were not fit to hunt any more, like to die, in fact.

OCTOBER 25th THURSDAY.

The meet was at Beckhead, Witherslack. On horseback were Miss Weston, Miss Drew on Handsome, Mr Dobson on Prince, Miss Heaton on her new horse, Miss White on Percy, Miss Hodgson on Arraby. A very wet day. The woods were drawn up to the piggaries. Four deer were seen to run up and over. Some hounds went up but all came back except one. A stag was footed in Pather pots and believed to have gone to Foulshaw. Hounds then never left the woods as no other deer went away. Very wet.

OCTOBER 29th MONDAY.

Meet at Rigmaden Bridge. On horseback were Miss Weston on Lionel, Mr Harry Dobson on Percy, Mr Bruce Rigg on Wizard, Miss Mary Rigg on Nettle, Miss D. Drew on Mick, Miss Mary Heaton on her new horse, Mr. Dick Heaton on Amber, Mr Locke King on Amazon, Mrs King, on Utile. Miss D. Crowdson on John With Miss H. Drew on Prince, Mr Barlow on Punch. A large hind was found in Frith Wood, which ran straight up the fell and over towards Dent. Owing mostly to the unfitness of their horses the field were unable to follow, but the hounds were collected Near Bullpot from Dent, no one having followed them.

NOVEMBER 1st THURSDAY.

A Lawn Meet at Kidside, by the kind invitation of Mr. Charles Wilson. The Hang Bridge deer was found just beyond the railway. The mounted company included, Miss Weston on Lionel, Mr Bruce Rigg on Wizard Miss Mary Rigg on Nettle, Mr Reynolds on Grumbles, Mrs Reynold on Tallulah, Mr John Heaton on Ponto, Miss Mary Heaton on her horse, Mr Martin Heaton on Amber, Mr Dick Heaton on Ashby, Miss Drew on Handsome, Miss D. Drew on Punch, Mr Harrison Broadley

Oct. 29th

The hunt servants wonder where the hounds have gone.

Vessle out of control.

The Listeners.

Miss Heaton's horse with a leg down.

Nov: 1st

The deer says goodbye to the hens.

Some people didn't know the country

Road hogs laughing at unfortunate cyclist.

Nov. 1st

Galloper. (the late)

Last but not least.

Handsome shows the way

The deer takes the railings onto the tar.

on Mr Guy Gardner's new horse, Mr Dobson on Scott, Miss Radcliffe
on Araby, Miss Diana While on Percy., Mr Alan North, on his
Father's horse, and Miss H. Drew on her bicycle - The deer
commenced by visiting Holme, and doing its usual
Tour of the Hen comps. It then ran North by the
railway and crossed the road ~~just~~ just south
of the Halehane Railway Bridge. It ran through the
cream of the country, crossed the road north of
the Duke of Cumberland, and under the Canal
in the beck. Here it was lost and unfortunately
not found again. If Mr Cropper had been there
they would probably have had another hunt, so
they say. It must have dodged back down the
beck when they were trying at Farleton foot.
Anyway it was back home at Elm field
that night. A certain gentleman who was
standing on the Canal Bridge saw where
it went to. but he wasnt telling anyone,
he said it was cruel, but however he seemed
to enjoy watching all the same.

NOVEMBER 5ᵗʰ MONDAY.

Meet at the station inn, Oxenholme. On horseback
were Miss Weston on Mick, Miss Drew on Handsome,
Mr Dobson on Scott, Miss Radcliff on Arraby, Sam Hodgson
on Prince, Miss Diana While on Percy, Mr Gaddum, M.H. Mr. Harrison
Broadley on Mr Gardner's horse, Mrs Locke King on Amazon, Mr. Bruce Rigg
on Wizard. Mr John Heaton on Ashby, Mr Martin Heaton on Amber,
Col. Cowdson on Punch, Mrs Cowdson on Ginger Wine,
Miss Deborah Cowdson on John Willy, Col. Oliver North, Miss
Somervell on Miss Bumbles, Miss Heaton on her new horse, Mr. Rutter
on Shelagh. The country was travelled by road and
lane to Lambrigs, north of the Sedbergh road.
The deer was found here, a hind, which ran
east, and turned south by Lily mere, and
after a heavy moorland day found refuge on
the island in Killington reservoir. Personally
I didn't see more than the first five minutes as
I overanticipated the course of the quarry, and
guided my transport towards Tebay where I lost
control of them and we only met the hunt when they had finished

Nov: 5th

The last I saw of hounds.

Within an ace of the
summit the ship loses way.

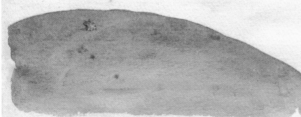

What I saw of the hunt.

A day in the bogs.

Collecting hounds by Killington Reservoir.

Nov: 8th

HA:HA! M3 STAGHOUNDS TODAY.

The Egyptian Police Horse.

WARE HARE

Nov: 12th.

A Press Photograph.

NOVEMBER 9th THURSDAY.

The meet was at Rigmaden Bridge, on a misty day nearly raining properly, and never fine, and snow on the top of Middleton Fell. The mounted company included Miss Worston on Lionel, Mr Cropper on Potato (nice to see him out again), Mrs Morden Rigg on Sir Lancelot (another first appearance) Col, Crewdson on Punch, Mr Dick Heaton on Amber, Miss Heaton, on Mr Jimmy Rutter on a novelty grey horse (believed to have been bought from the Egyptian Mounted Police. The Oxenholme Staghounds unfortunately had a blank day, but the Oxenholme Harriers I believe had several roustering hunts in the Foot hill woods about Middleton Hall, Synagogue wood and Northerdale gill, I dont know, I had gone home. It rained. The hunt Ball, Witherslack was that night.

NOVEMBER 12th MONDAY

The Hounds met at Hutton Bridge End, on a very fine still hunting morning. The mounted field, besides Miss Worston on

Lionel, ~~the~~ ~~mounted~~ ~~field~~ included:— Miss Drew on
Handsome, Miss D. Drew on Miss Weston's new Cob,
Mr Dotson on Prince, Miss Radcliff on Araby, Miss While
on Percy, Mrs Crowdson on John Willy, Col. Crowdson on Punch,
Mr Bruce Rigg, Miss Mary Rigg on Nettle, Miss Mary Heaton
on Clonmel, Mr Martin Heaton on Ponto, Mr Jimmy Rutter
on a grey horse, Miss Rutter on Shelagh?, a gentleman on Mabel?,
Mr John Heaton on Ashby, Miss Lees and her groom.
A deer was found (a hind) between New Hutton and
and the Kendal Sedbergh Road, and ran east
past the reservoir, over the moors by Lily Mere, to
Three Mile House, then turned back by Bendrigg to
the reservoir, where they checked. Either the same or
another deer was seen running up from the the
south west corner of the reservoir towards New Hutton
but no hounds followed it. Hounds ran on down towards
Lily mere to about the Black ~~Horse~~ Killington, then
turned back again to the reservoir. I, myself
only saw the deer running up from the reservoir,
from the hill behind 3. mile ho, and none of the main hunt

Nov: 12th

" A Bohireen', A Bohireen!" (From Heresay) | The Mule of my daughter.

A Lathering road race to avoid the bogs.

The Police horse guarding the reservoir

13

Nov: 15th

Wanted, a rider.

Wherever can she be.

Come what may

A matter of training
The end of a perfect day

NOVEMBER 15TH THURSDAY.

A great company of people assembled at the Kennels, Miss Weston appearing on her new cob. Others mounted were: Miss Drew on Handsome, Miss D. Drew on Mabel, Mr Cropper on Potato, Col. Crewdson on Punch, Mrs Crewdson on Ginger Wine, Miss Deborah Crewdson on John Willy, Mr. Bruce Rigg on Patrick, Miss Mary Rigg on Nettle, Col. Oliver North, on Caton, Mr John Heaton on Ponto, Miss Mary Heaton on Clonmel, Mr Dick Heaton on Amber, Mrs Morden Rigg on Sir Lancelot, Dalby on Dalham, Mr. James Reynolds on Grumbles, Mrs Reynolds on Tallulah, Mr. Harold Lee on Bobby, Mr. Dobson on Prince, A German gentleman on Percy, Mr. J. Rutter on a grey, Capt. Ashworth on Duke, Sherritt on Paul, Miss Lees and her groom, Mrs Wilson on Barney, *Miss Somerley on Bumble.* The local deer was looked for in Askrigg, and the surrounding country by Stainton, but not found, as it was lying among the turnips below the wood. A black buck was found in Bank's Planting, which ran over the fell to Rigmaden, up by the copses to Middleton Bridge, and back down the Middleton side of the valley to Rigmaden Bridge. Hounds were stopped at Grimes Hill. A rattling hunt.

NOVEMBER 19th MONDAY.

The hounds met at Old Town. Miss Weston road her new cob. Otherwise were Mr Cropper on Jenny Wren, Mr Dobson on Full measure, Miss Radcliffe on Araby, Miss D. Crawdson on John Willy, Col. Crowdson on Punch, Mrs Dorothy Heaton on Pixey, Mr John Heaton on Ponto, Miss Heaton on Clonmel, Mrs. Wilson on Barney, Miss Nees and her groom Miss Bickerstett on Grey Dawn, Mrs Morden Rigg on Sir Lancelot. Miss Somervell on Bumble. 7 deer, (5 hinds, 2 calves?) went away across the park from Underley, they made a circle up above Mansergh school, then down to the river again. They split, a hind and a calf going up river to Rigmaden Bridge. Hounds were lifted from where they had lost them by the river to the Bridge where they got away, and after some patchy work past Grimes Hill turned up by the copses, and onto Stony Park, across towards Banks Planting, and right handed to Black Essat. They had lost the hind on top and were chasing the calf. The got away again from Black Essat and ran over the end of Stony Park to the river again. Capital Sport

16

Nov. 19th

The Mothers Union, and

The hounds copying their formation.

Hounds being lifted to Rigmaden Bridge.

Mr Dobson sends his race horse home.

Going to the meet. The different effect of the lady's saddle.

Racing the deer out of Dallam Park.

Handsome does.

Fullmeasure does not.

NOVEMBER 22ⁿᵈ THURSDAY.

Crooklands was the meeting place of a great
company of horse people and foot people, including
Mr Cropper on Potato, Miss D. Drew on Handsome, Miss
Radcliffe on Arraby, Mrs. Heaton on Percy. Miss Diana White
on Fullmeasure, Mrs. Locke King on Amazon, Mr. John Heaton
on Ponto, Miss Heaton on Clonmel, Mr. Martin Heaton on Amber,
Mr Dick Heaton on Ashby, Miss Somervell on Bumble, Mr Rutter
on a grey, Mr North on Caton, Mr. Peter Dickinson on Cavk
Silver Rain, Mrs. Morden Rigg on Sir Lancelot, Miss Lees
and her groom, Captain Ashworth on Duke, Sherritt on Paul,
Miss Deborah Crowdson on Punch. Miss Weston was riding
Lionel. The lost Eskrigg-Derpthwaite deer had got into Dallam
Park, so Daniel and Warrington being selected as tufters
got it out by the ford at the Bertram corner.
Hounds were taken and got onto it just across
the road. It ran in a circle then crossed the
Milnthorpe-Burton road just south of Whasset, and
straight up to Milnthorpe station over the road
across the railway at the next bridge, and onto

10

Deepthwaite, across, east of Stainton to Eskrigg. Here it was lost, and after making a circle round towards Crosscrake, the line it was found again near Eskrigg and taken up and across the road to Stainton, where the deer was found and left in a little wood above the beck after a rattling days sport. A memorable hund.

NOVEMBER 26th MONDAY.

Meet was at Keepers Lodge, Dalton. Miss Weston rode her new chestnut cob. Besides were, Miss Drew on Handsome, Miss Radcliffe on Araby, Mrs Heaton on Percy, Mr Cropper on Potato, Miss While on Peter. Miss Somervell on Stumble, Mr John Heaton on Amber, Miss Heaton on Clonmell, Mr Alan North on Caton, Miss Lees and her groom, Mr Todd on a little black beast. An ancient stag, which had gone back to 9 prongs was routed from the great wood at Dalton, and crossed over to the ghyll, turned up it, then switched right, short of the Hutton Roof main road, and ran straight to the lune below Whittington, disturbing the Whittington coverts on the way. They all went to Capanwray, to Arkholme and round to Whittington, and no one followed it except miss Drew who tracked it.

20

Nov: 22nd

Mr Peter Dickinson giving his horse a lead.

Mrs Heaton goes to ground "She jump and jump till there was no breath left in her body."

Nov. 26th Monday.

Leave it to me and get on with your tracking.

Deer disturbing Whitting ton Coverts

NOVEMBER 29th THURSDAY

The meet was at Moorcock, Rigmaden. Miss Weston was riding Lionel. The mounted field were:- Mr Cropper on Jenny Wren, Mr John Heaton on Ashby, Mrs Wilson on Dolly, Miss Radcliffe on Araby, Mrs Morden Rigg on Dallam, Miss Mary Heaton on Clonmel, Col. Crewdson on Punch, Mrs Heaton on Percy, Mr Martin Heaton on Amber, Mr Harry Dobson on Betty, Mr Dick Heaton on Ponto, Miss Somervell on Rumble, Miss Lees & her groom, Miss Bickersteth on Grey Dawn, Miss Burra on her pony, and Miss H. Drew on Peter. A tame deer sitting just above the road on the right was shunned, and hounds were taken to the near end of Stoney Park, two hinds got away and the body of the pack followed them along the top and down to the lune by Hartriss Copses to Grimeshill. Four deer and four hounds are supposed to have run away north, certainly four hounds were lost. The hind ran south to Rigmaden Bridge, and crossed to the right bank again at

23

Bainsbank, and along the right bank till it crossed the river into the north corner of Underley park. We ran straight across the Park to the gardens, to across the river into the gardens and out again the other side, across the South Park to the seed fields, and across the river just south of casterton hall, and the deer was bayed in the river by Kirby. The turned out however, and after making a circle up to the road by casterton flall, crossed the river, and made up bank, along by Underley Park wood, along the bank. Hounds lost it just north of Underley Park, and were taken on to just south of Rigmaden, where they struck it, and after being stopped and taken past the Mansion were put on again just north, and ran it down to the river where they left the deer as the creatures seemed definitely to have taken a fancy to the water, and Otter Hounds would have been very Handy. Rare Sport.

Nov. 29th

"Only amatuers with us today"   New style.

"Can I come Harry?"   "Ay! Come on Albert"

Deer in the river near Kirby   Betty showing that
playing at otters.   "she can lep yet"

Dec: 3ª

Dishon, harbouror showing fresh slot it has taken all day to find.

They're away!

Helpful Information, for the huntsman
"They have gone yon way"

Caton trying to get
through a stone wall.
(From hearsay from the
rider's enemies)

Far Drew qualifying
mr Dobson's race horse
for him.

DECEMBER 3rd MONDAY.

The meet was at Slackhead. Mr Cropper, riding Potato was acting as master as Miss Weston was away doing Politics in London. Others were, Miss Drew on Handsome, Miss D. Crewdson on John Willy, Mr M. Haslam on Ashby, Miss Bentley on Peter, Mr Dobson on Fullmeasure, Miss Clark on Betty, Col. O. North on Caton, Mr Tony & Mr Peter Dickenson with Silver Rain and Mottle, Miss Lees and her groom. Robinson with 2 horses, 2 other horses, and Miss H. Drew on her bicycle. Underlaid was drawn blank, and Thrang End wood and Hale Moss. News was then got of all the deer having been seen that day on Arnside Moss. It was drawn blank, but they were found in the outskirts of Challon Hall wood about 3'6.d. and something went away. with **4½ couple** to Leighton Marsh and on to the Marble Quarrys. A stag took 1 couple back to Brackenthwaite, and the rest hunted a little hind over to Arnside knot and down to the sea at New Barnes Bay, and up again, leaving her on the knot at dusk in a fog.

DECEMBER 6ᵗʰ THURSDAY.

The meet was at Middleshaw, on a showery day.
The country was very wet. Miss Weston was back and
riding Ben. The field included:- Mr Cropper on Jenny
Wren, Miss Drew on Handsome, Col. Crewdson
on Punch, Mrs Crewdson on Ginger Wine, Miss D. Crewdson
on John Willy, Mrs King on Amazon, Mr King on Utile, Mr John
Heaton on Amber, Miss Mary Heaton on Clonmel, Miss Somervell
on Miss Bumble, Mr Rutter on Mabel. The deer, which had
been among some sheep about Middleshaw was separated,
and hounds got away fine very quickly. They ran
in a circle towards Millholme, then made north,
turning over Craker Fell to Killington Reservoir. Then
ran east along the south shore then turned down
into the country again by Brundrigg to Middleshaw
The deer crossed the main road just west
of Middleshaw and well ahead of hounds. They
found it again and ran a little way south
towards Cockerigg, where they were stopped, all
except wagtail who chased it to Holmscales. Where she was caught.
the deer going on up towards Hutton Bridge end.

Dec. 6th

The Wren on her toes,
(The dreadful effect of a horsebox?)

Away up the plough.

Putting on time, while the hounds
catch up a bit.

Juvenile riot. (Int turnips
goin (oozyer)

Wagtail feeling independant.

Mr. Cropper hunting for hound.

29

December 10th.

Miss Weston, M.S.H, on her chestnut cob, Ben, wearing her new red jacket.

Woodland hurdling near the kennels.

DECEMBER 10th MONDAY.

Hounds met at Plough Inn, Lupton. Miss Wiston in her new
red jacket rode her cob. Others mounted were Miss D. Drew
on Handsome, Mr Dobson on Betty, Col. Crewdson on Punch.
Miss Crewdson on John Willy, Mrs King on Utile, Mr King on
Kendal Kid, Mr John Heaton on Ashby, Miss Heaton on Clonmel,
Mr Martin Heaton on his new, chaser. Miss Lees and her man,
Miss Somervell on Miss Bumble, Mr Chris Willink on Mick,
Mr Rutter on Mabel, Mr Todd, and a chap on a chestnut,
No quarry was ventd, as Gracie from Lupton and
Farleton, and Emily from Holmscales were on Holiday —

DECEMBER 13th THURSDAY.

The meet was at Old Town. Miss Drew was riding
Ashby. I believe they found late in the after noon at
Black Essex and had a quite good hunt. See the Gazette.

DECEMBER 17th MONDAY.

Hounds met at Gilpin Bridge. The mounted limited
company was Col. Crewdson on Punch? Mr John Heaton on
Ashby, Mr Dobson on Fulmeasure, Mr Alan Dobson
on Scott, Miss Margaret Hodgson on Peter. A big stag

81

was found in the wood under Whit barrow scar, and it ran over to the moss below Halecote, where it sent off two hinds and stayed, the hinds giving a ran gallop down to Meathrop, along the shore and up the cut to Foulshaw moss, and hounds were stopped at High Foulshaw. (This is Heresay)

DECEMBER 20ᵗʰ THURSDAY

The hounds met at Moorcock, Rigmaden. Miss Drew rode her grey, and ~~Mr Dalton~~ Mr Philip Scott, rode Miss Birkett's Retty, Mr Cropper was mounted, but for the rest I cannot remember exactly, excepting Mr Edward Wilson, who is an example to the rising generation. A hind was found on Stony Park, and it ran down to the river via the copses, along through Rigmaden Big wood to the Holmes, where it crossed, and went nearly to Barbon, but was headed, and turned north, and after running parallel with the lane for a bit, it swung west and over the main road, and the race course, and down the river towards Underley. Some people seem to have had a rare lot of obstacles.

32

Dec: 17th

The stag makes "it worth his while" to
set the pace instead of himself, who will take their place.

Dec: 20th

Showing them how.

Miss Drew and Mr Scott
make an "oath to follow"
hounds wherever they go.

Handsome does.

Some unexpected water.

Dec: 24th

There was a notable following of children.

Handsome show- the world how to jump walls.

"I feel my young thoroughbred strain down the ride."

Young monster, having told old monster to give her a lead, laughs at her peril.

Tally Ho! at last. The four deer on Burn's Pasture.

They't away! The monsters trying to make a getaway in a bog.

CHRISTMAS EVE.

A dark meet at Middleshaw, with a great holiday company including Major Cropper on Potato, Mr Anthony Cropper on Jenny Wren, Colonel Benson their guest would have hunted had his horse Betty not gone lame at the meet, Miss Drew on Handsome Miss D. Drew on Fullmeasure, Mr Peter Ballinik on Mick, Mr Gardner on Paul, Miss Radcliffe on Arraby, Mr John Heaton on Amber, Mr Cresswell on Kendal Kid, Mrs Morden Rigg, and many others, including the monsters embarking their hunting career en bloc. After vain search of the Holmscales directions, and also the country just north of Hutton Bridge and, Banks Plantin was also drawn Blank, so hounds were threatened with Stony Park, but LO! When the Rigmaden Road was reached, there were four hinds on Burn's Pasture. The hounds were loosed, and ran at the deer, which being routed decided to give sport, so ringing north through Black assart, she turned

left handed over the tops, along, then
down to the Moorcock road through
the dead plantin, across, and down to
the river at the Holmes, and along to
Underley Park. At the far end of the Holmes
there was a check in the river, and three
fresh deer got up and took all the hounds
except 2 couple, back the other side of
the river a rare dance over the race-course,
finally ending up somewhere near Underley.
The 2 couple of diehards hunted slowly on
across the park, and on down the fields
by the road to Casterton Hall, where they
recrossed the river into Underley Park, and
hounds were all stopped by the whip
who turned up except one which hunted
the deer on into the rhododendrons behind
the mansion, where these stayed, but one
went on through the river and across the park,
with the one hound after it, but it too was stopped

Dec: 24th

Old Prentz gets left
behind at a gate,
and catches up thus.

Some people where foolish enough to
give away their horses, and others had more
sense than to refuse a good offer.

The monsters
hunting en bloc.

Fresh deer, (on left) cause confusion.

Diehards hunting the first deer with 2 couple of hounds.

Much welcome help was
got in stalking and tracing.

Unfortunate plight of old monster, who
having had to dismount to shut a gate, find
her horse has assumed mammoth proportions

They're away. the horse finds
it easier than the genuine pushbike.

But its easier down the Tar

Miss N. Coopper whipping in to her father

EVERSLEY WOMAN'S

MARSH ORDEAL

This is the only official picture.

DECEMBER 27th THURSDAY

A great feasting meet at Dallam Tower, with
a rare collection of Sportsmen and women on
horseback, foot, bicycles, and in motor cars.
The master rode her chestnut and Mr Chris Willink Rock Buck,
also Mr Cropper on Potato, Mr Anthony Cropper on Jennylina
Col. Benson on Mabel, Miss Nancy Cropper on Peter, Miss Radcliffe on Araby, Miss Drew on Handsome. Miss Bentley on Bloom
                                                         Miss Clark
Mr Martin Heaton on Pontini, Mr Dick Heaton on Amber, Miss Heaton
on Batty
on Clonmel, Miss Somervell on Bumble, Mrs Bruce Riggs, Mrs
Morden Rigg, Mr Cresswell on Amazon, and others ad. lib.
Hounds were taken to Underlaid, and a stag went
away at the south end pretty soon, and crossed
Thrang end, passed by Yealand Smithy, along the
bottom, and went up across Leighton Hall Park onto
Wharton Crag, He turned at the top and passing
down through the wood, he crossed the lane at
the bottom, and followed the beck across to the level crossing
then turning right he went up and left the water just
north of the causeway, and stopped in a little wood just

across the road. The hound lost it by the level crossing, and were collected there, as the water was very cold and they were getting chilled off. Woodbine was drowned.

NEW YEAR'S DAY. TUESDAY.

The meet at Leighton on the 31st Dec. was postponed until this day, owing the the funeral of Mrs. Bill Saunders. The Kennels was the meeting place of horse and hound, and a great company assembled including a great many people from the Vale of Lune. Harness Miss Drew took her grey to meet them at the first cover, but then took him home to rest preparatory to Thursday's hunt. The visitors included Mr and Mrs Harrison-Broadley, Mr and Mrs Reynolds, Mr Harold Lee, and Miss Delphine Reynolds on Betty. Others were Mr Anthony Copper on Jenny Wren, Potato, Mr Chris Willink on Mick, Mr Eric Wilson. etc. They tried to get the Carnforth deer to leave the wood above Levens Park, but they didn't manage to, and it got into the Park, so they left it for fear of killing the fallow. deer. They eventually found the Mill Holme deer after drawing upstream from Cockriggs, and seem to have had a cracking hunt.

40

Dec: 27th

The deer which started the day as a young stag, left the marsh looking like this

All during the terrors of the ordeal it stood listening, "standing between two trees".

Jan: 1st

Young bloods preparing for a gallop.

Miss Drew taking her horse home as a protest against the tame deer having been allowed to jump into the park.

Timely aid from the visiting master.

Jany: 3rd

Intelligent Hunters hollooing hounds away in the fog, so as to let the horsebacks know that they are not running the usual way.

In and out.

Deer waiting to be hunted, in case the other deer should be lost.

Hardriding set looking for the biggest place

42

JANUARY 3ʳᵈ THURSDAY

A dark determined meet with shoulder to shoulder
eating and drinking at Rigmaden - Besides Miss
weston, Major Cropper was mounted, Miss Drew on Betty,
Mr Johnson on Handsome, Mr Eric Wilson on Barney,
Col. Crowdson on Punch, Miss Crowdson on her new horse, a friend
on Arraby, Mr Christlethink on Dick, Mr John Heaton on Ashby,
Miss Heaton on Cromwell, Mr Martin Heaton, Mr Dick Heaton on Amber,
Miss While on Punch, and others. The mist descended
onto the tops. Hounds were taken up to Stoney Park,
and a hind went away west, crossing the
road where the lane from 3 Mile Ho. joins it, and
mounting the moor tops, turned left towards Barton
house and Kitmere, and then turned down towards
Moorcock, and crossed the Moorcock road south of
the cottage, then after ringing around the big wood
turned north west again, and crossed the Moorcock Road
just north of the cottage, and running towards Crosslands was lost up
by Banks Plantin. 4 hinds were found near the Track End, and having
divided on Burn's Pasture, two were hunted over Stoney Park, down
the copses to the river below Gill Foot, where hounds were stopped

43

JANUARY 7ᵗʰ MONDAY.

The meet was at Witherslack Hall, and was well attended by spectators. Miss Weston rode Lionel, also were Miss Drew on Handsome, Col. Crewdson on Punch, Mr. Dobson on Poppy, Miss Bentley on Mr Brown, Mr Bentley on Full measure, Sir Ian Rory Hay Stuart-Richardson on Punch, Mr Michael Stanley on Joseph, Miss Stanley on a white pony, Miss H. Drew on Woodcock, Mrs Morden Rigg on Sir Lancelot, Mr Alan Dobson on Sunray, and one or two more. A hind was hunted most of the day, with intervals of roe from time to time. Hounds were hunting all day up and down the woods, but never left them.

JANUARY 10ᵗʰ THURSDAY.

Hounds met at Lupton School. Miss Weston rode Ben, Mr Cropper on Potato, Miss Nancy Cropper on Arraby, Mr Christopher on Mick, Mr Phil. Scott on Prince, etc. They found two hinds near Tosca which ran towards Kirkby, and then they turned left handed. They were now hunting the calf so they were stopped near Keastwick, and they tried Mansergh Hall but nothing more was found.

44

Jan 7th

The Fat Drew being ushered to her unfortunate mount.

Sir Ian joins the pony club.

Jan: 10th

"Go on Sweenie, you'll be late." The
little monster refuses Miss Radcliffe's horse. But not for long.

45

Narrow escape of hunting motorists

Old ten-prongs off to the Lakes —

Why the — cant you keep to your own — country

Handsome shunning the "gap of deception"

46

JANUARY 14th MONDAY.

The meet was at the Keeper's Lodge Dalton. The mounted followers included ~~Mr Cropper~~, Miss D. Drew on Handsome, Mr Dobson on Punch, Miss Radcliffe on Arraby, Miss Heaton on Clonmell, Mr John Heaton on Amber, Col. Piers North on Crummock, Col. O. North on Caton, Mrs. M. Rigg on Sir Lancelot, Dalby on Dallam, Mr. George Dickinson (2) Miss Lees (2). The Big Wood was drawn, and two great stags got on the move. One with ten prongs went away with 6 couple of hounds towards Dalton Hall, and after ringing round the Park went away over the hill to Burton, down by Holme across the flats to the woods at the north end of the Mossdale straight. Here it crossed the road, and skirting Hale Moss, passed over through Thrang, Brackenthwaite and Arnside Tower Moss, over the ~~hurst~~ flats below Hazelslack tower, to the Estuary, where it crossed to Ulpha. It went on up over Cattwell Fell to Windermere. The other stag with the rest of the hounds and all the people went by Whittington, Newton, across the hume to Thurland and hounds were stopped just before Black Burton, to avoid running into fresh deer. A rattling hunt —

47

JANUARY 17ᵀᴴ THURSDAY.

The meet was at Hutton Bridge End. Mr Cropper on Jenny Wren was acting master. Mounted were, Miss Drew on Handsome, Miss Radcliffe on Arraby, Miss Mary Heaton on Clonmell, Mr Dick Heaton on Amber, Col. Pim North on Crummock, Mr John Heaton on Ashby, Miss Somervell on Miss Rumble, Mr Cresswell on Kendal Kid, Mr Harry Dobson on Scot, Miss V. Cropper on Peter, *Punch*, and Miss H. Drew on Prince, Mr Teddy Wilson and Co. Mrs Crewdson, Miss D. Crewdson, Mrs Bruce Rigg, and others. The Wood by Hood Ridding was drawn blank, so was Bank's Plantin, but Mr Cropper 'spied four deer on Barkin Moor near the Moorcock road, and hounds were laid onto these. They ran along the tops to Moorcock where they divided up, two going on down to the river near the Holmes, where hounds were stopped and taken back to Moorcock, and laid onto a single hind. They hunted down to the river at Carradice, and crossed the valley nearly to Synagogue

48

Jan: 17th

Tallyho 2 miles away. The acting master gets us a hunt.

Handsome meets his match

"Put not your trust in Princes" Unfortunate accident shortening the lives of all concerned, including the clothes.

Piteous spectacle of monster loosing its nerve on seeing that its friend, to whom it has trusted to guide it to safety on the bogs is now leading it back to the fatal rhododendrons. !!

Jan: 17th

Difficulties of striking an aquaintance when Trotting in a wind.

"Don't wait for me, the old man's lost a shoe." The monsters are packed off by Miss Radcliffe to follow Col. Crewdson.

The Colonel to the rescue. The other monster is floored.

Jan: 21st

Miss N. Cropper trying to look as though she meant to go as fast as we did.

Wretched monster dying after bicycling 7 miles in ¾ hrs.

Righteous indignation of farmer Hill on finding that the hunt has left the gate open and (50) his cows are in danger from the marsh.

wood, then swung round and made across to Bainsbank racecourse. Then she crossed the river, and made up to the moors again by Rigmaden, and down again to the river where hounds were stopped. There were no followers on the last up and down circuit other then the huntservants. The monsters got badly lost on the second descent, and decided that they needed teaching about hunting.

JANUARY 21st MONDAY.

The meet was at Yealand Smithy. Miss Weston rode her Chestnut, Miss Nancy Cropper on Potato, Miss Lees (2), Mr Dobson on Hoppy, Mrs Morden Rigg, and several others. A stag was pushed out of Deepdale, and ran across Leighton Hall Park to Grizedale, where he turned back towards the Smithy, and on over Thrang to Brakenthwaite and Underlaid, to the Sea near Sandside where he took to the water and crossed, but hounds were stopped.

51

JANUARY 24th THURSDAY.

A dark meet at the Kennels. Miss Weston rode Lionel, and others were Miss Drew on Handsome, Miss D. Drew on Ben, Miss Lees (2), Mrs Norden Rigg (2), Miss Diana While on "Bacchus" (Punch), Miss Radcliffe on Arraby, Mr. Dobson on Scott, Mr Alan Dobson on Fullmeasure, Mr John Heaton on Ashby, Mr. Martin Heaton on Garbo, Mr Dick Heaton on Amber, Miss Mary Heaton on Clonmell, and some Dickinsons, etc. Hounds were taken by Birkrigg and Hyth House to Cockrigg, and after trying the country at the back of Helm the deer was found in a field near Cockrigg, and ran north by Middleshaw, made a ring in the country north of it, and ran up to the Reservoir, and back round the south breast of Cracer fell, up past New Hutton to the Sedbergh road at the Gin Shop, and over it onto Bensonknot, where Hounds were stopped after a short but cracking hunt. This was the Carnforth deer which had been promoted.

JANUARY 28th MONDAY

The meet would have been at the Lyth Valley Hotel (Plough Inn), but they were stopped by FROST, the only day that they have so far missed this season

Jan: 24th

Mr. Dobson does some harbouring for Miss Weston

It's wonderful what a few oats can do.

Miss Lees setting the pace.

Racehorse ignoring a stubborn stopgap.

Handsome proving the greatness of his Irish Ancestors

Jany. 31st

Mr Dobson on "Old Prentz" preparing to "have a go."

And the unknown man was there having walked all the way along the blue road.

Feb: 4th

Hind on the move

setting its course for Grange.

Push bike riders holding their own down Arnside Knot.

54

JANUARY 31ˢᵗ THURSDAY.

Hounds met at Old Town. Miss Weston rode Lionel, Miss Drew on Handsome, Miss D. Drew on Ben, Miss Radcliffe on Araby, Mr Dobson on ~~Loppy~~ Prince, Miss Diana While on Bacchus, Miss Bidercstath on Grey Dawn, Miss D. Crawdson, Col. & Mrs Crawdson, Mich.ll.ck, Col North (Views), Heatons (4), and sundry. They found some deer at Underley which took them sharp up to Terry Bank, and they didn't find again all day —

FEBUARY 4ᵗʰ MONDAY.

Meet at Hazelslack Tower. Miss Weston on her chestnut, Mr Cropper on Potato, Miss Drew on Handsome, Michers(?) Miss Deborah Crawdson on Punch, Mr Dobson on Loppy, Mr martin Heaton on Garbo, Mr Dick Heaton on Amber, Mr Alan North on Caton, Mr Peter and Mr tony Dickinson on Prince and Silver Rain, Mrs Morden Rigg on Sir Lancelot. The Fat-dorns on their bicycles. A hind was found in the wood above Arnside Tower, and she ran down onto Arnside Park, and after circling around the woods made down past High Barns Bay to the sea, and crossed over to ~~Arnside~~ Grange. Hounds

55

did their best to cross too but were got back,
and taken to Taddy Hill where some deer had
been seen. After trying the bottom of Underlaid for a bit they hunted them slowly
across the road, and put them up again behind
~~Arnside~~ Hazelslack Tower, when they divided, one running
back to Underlaid, on through Brakenthwaite,
over Thrang End when they were stopped.

FEBUARY 7ᵗʰ THURSDAY.

An eating meet at Burnside, Barbon, with the hospitality
of Mrs Gibson. Miss Weston rode Lionel. Miss Drew on
Handsome, Mr Dobson on Punch, Miss Radcliffe on Arraby.
Miss Somervell on Bumble, Miss Bickersteth on Grey Dawn, Mrs Morden Rigg
on Sir Lancelot, Mr John Heaton on Ashby. Miss Mary Heaton on Amber.
Col. Piers North on Crummock, Mrs Teddy Wilson and co, and one or two others.
The manor woods were drawn and a hind was
roused and ran along the wall side in the wood
on the south of the glyll, and after crossing the middle
drive, turned north, and crossing the glyll broke cover
near the N.W. corner of the wood, and out onto the

56

FEb:4½2

Miss Weston warming up a rheumatiky old hound after calling her pack off the deer which had swum to Grange.

Miss Drew teaching her good young hunter how to walk over wire.

A change of mounts. (welcome?)

Feb:7½

Tallyho Point Blank!

Miss Drew being helped out of the country by an old accomplice.

Deer with a beautiful soul choosing a really nice bit of country

57

Feb: 7th

Miss Radcliffe receiving a gallant lead over an old enemy.

"T'other side of th'road's vacant, John." Col. John proceeds to try and occupy it.

Feb: 11th

Hopeless optimist looking for a deer in Paradise.

"There must be plenty of places for the stag to hide."

It was not by fog alone that he was troubled.

The beginning of the end.

58

fell. She ran along the fell about as far as Synagogue Wood, then came down and kept above the railway as far as Middleton Bridge, where she came down and ran down the river to Rigmaden Bridge. Here she waited until hounds were brought up, and then she made out, and crossing the top end of Bainsbank made straight back to Barbon. A fresh deer was roused, and the two made north together along the fell and coming down off the fell about Middleton hall, ran on above the road and the railway, then turned back after about half a mile or so beyond Middleton Bridge, and hounds were stopped at water meeting.

FEBUARY 11th MONDAY.

Meet at the Kennels. Miss Weston rode Lionel. Mr Cropper on Jenny Wren, Miss Drew on Handsome, Miss D.Drew on Ben, Mr John Heaton on Ashby. Capt. E. Prior-Palmer on Amber, Miss Heaton on Clonmell, Mr Martin Heaton on Garbo, Miss Diana While on Punch, Col. Piers North on Crummock, Mr Dobson on Hoppy. and some Crowdsons and others. A thick day. Cockrigg was drawn blank, and the country round Mill holme was drawn blank for that deer, though it was reported to have been sitting behind a hedge all the time. Eventually the tame deer was hunted round Benson Knot, but never went away — very disappointing.

KILL.

FEBUARY 14ᵗ THURSDAY.

Hounds met at Moorcock Rigmaden in a sleet storm.
Mr Cropper rode Jenny Wren, Mr Teddy Wilson and Co.
Miss Radcliffe on Arraby, Mr Dobson on Peter, Mr Bruce
Rigg on Wizard, Miss Mary Rigg on Nettle, Mrs Somervill on
Bumble, Miss Crowdson on her new horse, Mrs Morden Rigg on Sir lancelot,
Miss Mary Heaton on Clonmell, Mr Dick Heaton on Amber.?
A deer was found on Stoney Park, it was a young stag
and he ran down towards the river, then up
again crossing the road near the cotage at the top of the
frist hill north of Rigmaden. He then ran along above the
Big wood, and jumping out into the country sorth of Rigmaden
he fell in some wire and hurt himself. Then down to the
river at the holmes. They found him here and tried to
drive him away from the river as it was too big to cross.
He ran north along the river, and they caught
him in it just north of Rigmaden Bridge. He
floated below the Bridge, and when the hounds had all been
called off, Mr Cropper shot him under the bank with a shot gun,
it having been impossible to shoot him swimming with the pistol

Feb. 14th Thursday.

The travellers in Miss Weston's Automobile have a splendid view of hounds crossing the road.

"A good un to go." awarded to Miss M. Rigg.

The hunted deer coming the "most appalling of purlers."

Coursing the deer away from the flooded river to save the hounds.

Fierce hounds baying in the river.

Mr. Cropper lying in wait with the pistol

Arraby as lame as a tree, and nobody's sweetheart, for Harry said: "If he's no good to her, he's no good to me".

Miss Weston doing her duty as the master is bound to do.

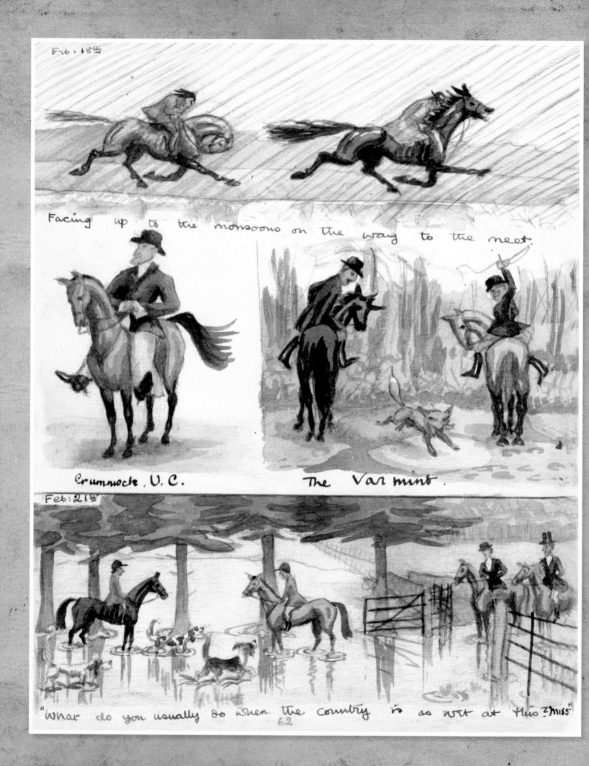

FEBUARY 18th MONDAY.

The meet was at the Keeper's lodge, Dalton, and after a filthy wet morning until about 11.30, it got fine. Miss Loveter rode Ben. Miss Drew on Handsome, Mr Alan North on Caton, Col. Piers North on Cerinnmock, Col. John Heaton on Ashby, Mr Dobson on Loppy, Mr Alan Dobson on Scott, Miss Clarke on Peter, Mr Harold Lee on Tallulah, Miss Mary Heaton on Clonmell. After trying through Hale Moss and Thrang End, nothing could be found, so hounds were taken to Underlaid, which was also drawn blank. Eventually two hinds were found in the ghyll below, and they ran out by the bungalows and rough lots and Cold Well to Brackenthwaite, and back to Underlaid. Then they did it again.

FEBUARY 21st THURSDAY.

Meet at Rigmaden Bridge, Miss Weston on Lionel, Miss D. Drew on Ben, Mr. Martin Heaton on Garbo, Mr Dick Heaton on Amber, Col. J. Miss Bickersteth on Grey Dawn, Miss D. Gawdson on her Horse. The country was mighty wet, No deer were found in Synagogue, and went on the fell, where the ground was in bog, and the river was in flood, so they went home.

63

FEBUARY 25ᵗʰ MONDAY.

Meet at Yealand Smithy, besides Miss Weston who
Mr Dobson on Scott hoppy, and later on Peter, Miss Bentley
on Scott, Mr Alan Dobson on Peter; Miss Radcliffe on Arraby,
Miss D. Crewdson, Mr Martin Heaton on Garbo, Mr Dick Heaton
on Amber, Miss Mary Heaton on Clonmell;? Mrs Brook, Misihees(2),
Mr Dickinson (2), Hounds were taken to Grizedale to
draw, but it was empty, so they tried Potts woods, and a
hind went away towards Laighton. She turned in a
ring, left-handed over the hill, and down to the marsh, where
hounds were stopped. A young stag did the same, so hounds were
taken round and got onto him again at Silverdale station. He ran
by Challon Hall and Brakenthwaite across Arnside Tower Moss to
Black Dyke, and crossed the estuary to Foulshaw. Hounds
were collected on Foulshaw Moss, where they had lost him.

FEBUARY 28ᵗʰ THURSDAY.

Hounds met at Barbon village. Miss Weston rode Lionel.
Mr John Heaton on Ashby, Miss D. Drew on Handsome, Miss Bickersteth
on grey Dawn, Mrs Wilson on Barney. Mr Teddy Wilson and Co., Miss Burn,
Mr J. Reynolds on Tallulah, Miss Mary Rigg on Nettle, Mr Dalby

Unpleasant situation for Sir Lancelot.

A good hound hunt.

A promising handful of amatuers.

Leu in there! "66 Terrific find.

on Sir Lancelot, Mr Dickinson (2). Miss H Drew
on Scott, A deer was found in the Manor woods,
and crossing the beck, ran straight up Casterton
Fell into the mist. Then turning right handed
made a circle in the country by Whelprigg,
then turned up again onto the fell, and coming
down the Bullpot road opposite the manor, crossed
the ghyll at the low end of the Manor woods,
and turning left ran straight across the
country to Bainsbank, then turned up the
river at Rigmaden Bridge, and lost it opposite
Grimes Hill, The huntservants were lost, so Miss
Weston collected hounds, and after trying the
country round Drybeck, and Gill Foot, up to Rigmaden
as nothing could be found, hounds were taken home.

MARCH 4th MONDAY.

Meet at Slackhead. Miss Weston on Lionel, Mr Cropper on
Potato, Miss Drew on Handsome, Miss D. Drew on Ben. The country
near Storth was drawn, and several deer were roused, but
gather it was a very woodland day. I was away and I
nld find nothing in the paper, so ask someone who was there.

MARCH 9th SATURDAY.

Meet at Gilpin Bridge. Two deer were found in Whitbarrow End. Hounds were stopped at the Estuary as one ran straight there, and were taken to where the other had crossed Ulpha lane for Meathop. They ran through Meathop and Halecote mosses to the Winster and back to Foulshaw. After ringing around the moss the broke out again over to Meathop and down to the Estuary, and the deer crossed, but hounds were stopped by viaduct.

MARCH. 16th SATURDAY.

Hounds met at Rigmaden Bridge. Miss Weston rode Ben. Others mounted were Miss Drew on Handsome, Mr Dobson on Scott, Miss Bickersteth on Grey Dawn, Miss Smith, Miss Wilson on Barney, Mr John Heaton on Ashby, Col. O. North on Caton, and happen another one or two. Hounds were taken right up the fell north of Northerdale Ghyll, and a deer was found on top. It ran over towards Dent, but never went down into the Dent Valley, then turned back and down the fell end to Middleton Bridge, where it crossed, and continued

Follow the leader. (or jump the wall)   Up the old Bainsbank water splash.

The hounds successfully carry off a well organized practical joke, for by luring A. Sims into a thicket they are able to separate him from his horse and abduct it. March 20th

Ten prongs swearing as he leaves the wood after using the drawing off ios to eight prongs and twelve prongs.

along down the river till Drybeck, where it waited in the country below the road till hounds came up. There were two hinds here, I expect there had been all the time. They ran straight up by the copses onto Stoney park, then turned left handed along the heights, through Rigmaden Big wood, down to the river at Flesh Beck. Here most of the pack lost it, but about 2 couple had gone on to Underley. So the rest of the pack were lifted to Underley Gardens. Here the other hounds were found, but ~~were~~ had lost, the deer, so after trying round as it was wet and nearly dark and nothing could be found hounds were taken home.

MARCH 20th WEDNESDAY.

A fine meet at Witherslack Post Office. Miss Weston rode Ben. Others were Miss Drew on Handsome, Mr Cropper on Potato, Miss Radcliffe on Arraby, Mr Dobson on Punch, Mr John Heaton on Ashby and one or two more. Three great stags had been harboured in a spinney near

91.

Thornmisty, so hounds were taken there, and
one of the three was roused, while the other two
never stirred. He ran straight up towards
Simpson Ground, then turning left handed. crossed
down just north of the Towtop road, and over
the cross roads across Halecote moss to the main
road, and over Meathop Moss to the sea at
Ulpha. The tide was in so he didnt cross.
but turned back left handed up the cut through
Foulshaw moss, and over the main road and
across to the gilpin just north of Gilpin
Bridge. Here they lost him, and although they
tried up the river as far as the toll Bar
road very nearly, they found nothing so hounds
were taken home after a short but working day.

MARCH 25ᵗʰ MONDAY.

A great meet at Yealand Smithy. Miss Weston
was on Ben. Others mounted included Mr Harold Lijson-
Lee (Farmer) on Bobby, Colonel Crewdson on Punch, Miss
D. Crewdson on her new horse, Mr Eric Wilson on one of

march: 20ᵗʰ

The Spirit of his ancestors

But all except Mr. John Heaton who had already jumped and Mr. Dobson and the huntsmen who were already round, all looked for the way round and so missed the hunt.

Handsome: "This is how I would do it."

"Dash it, I dont remember it being as wide as that."

march: 25ᵗʰ

A walk over for others but ys give me 'whoop in' every time.

"sit down, and dont get so excited."

Miss Lees' horses and her groom on the other, Mr John Heaton on Amber, Miss Mary Heaton on Clonmell, Mr Dick Heaton on Punch, and two of their lady guests on Loppy and Arraby, Miss Smith and Mr Smith, Miss Bentley on Scott, Miss Darlington, Mr Robinson and his boy, and Handsome carrying the Fat Drew. Hounds were taken to the woods on the s-w side of Wharton crag, but as nothing was found there they were taken on to Potts woods. No good, so they tried down towards Leighton Park, and it was footed out of here, and hounds owned a line from here down to Grizedale wood. Hounds were put into the wood, but nothing was found so they were taken back to try again near the marks, but it was a failure so they moved on to Deepdale, and Tallyho! A great stag and a hind set off down to the marsh, and crossing over ran over Thrang End to Underlaid.

75

They kept along the top side till they came
to the Beetham Road then instead of crossing
onto Haverbrack they turned back along
the fields below Underlaid for a bit, then
up the middle, and along and out again at
the south end. Here the deer went out
on the same route but about a field
apart parallel, and made for the marsh Through
Brackenthwaite. The hind crossed the marsh
with one hound, and went back to Grizedale.
But the stag turned back, and ran back
through Brackenthwaite to Challon Hall
where hounds were stopped. One hound
put up 4 hinds and a young stag in
Brackenthwaite, and hunted them over
Thrang lots to Thrang woods. Here they
divided, two going to the moss, and three
going left across the road towards Underlaid
they divided again, one going nearly to County Beck Farm.
and the other two disapeared and the hound was stopped.
By the end of the day this country was thick with
deer.

76.

109

March 20.

Some parts of the Oxenholme country are very rough, and a a clever horse is needed.

The great beast is roused at last.

Over t'bally fence, John."

Never above his hocks the whole way.

The bravest man and the least valuable horse are sent across to test the sands. 78

Some places would give even Tom Mix something to think about.

MARCH 30ᵗʰ SATURDAY

A meet at Witherslack Post Office again, Miss Weston's horse was ill so she was not riding. Mr John Hinton on Ashby was told off to act for her. Others were Mr Dobson on Punch, Miss Drew on Handsome, The Fat Drew on Scott, Miss Radcliff on Araby, Mrs Reynolds on Tallulah, Mr Martin Heaton on Cloud, Mr Smith and Miss Smith, Miss Brook, and another lady. Hounds were taken straight to the wood near Thorpinsty where the deer were found before, as they were supposed still to be there. They were not found there however, so they went up to heff wood and tried down, and hunted a goat down to the road. They then tried the wood just above Thorpinsty Farm, but it was no good, so they went along the upper road, and tried the north brow of the open fell between the two roads, and just as they were getting down to the road up jumped the great stag which they had hunted before, with ten prongs, and away he went

79

along the Fell foot to the crossroads where
he crossed into the fields between Halecote
moss and the road. He made straight across
the main-road, over the edge of Ulpha Moss
to the water at Ulpha Point, and as the
tide was out he went straight across
the sands to Sandside, and hounds went
too and the people who were there, and struck
off the line just across and away they went
along the turf, over the railway and across
the flats towards Arnside tower but turned
left after crossing the Arnside-Yealand road, and over
Arnside moss to Challon Hall, and over into Brackenthwaite,
by Halvswater over to Leighton. But the hounds
divided in Brackenthwaite 6½ couple going off
with hind fresh put up round to Underland.
Hounds were collected in Brackenthwaite and
round about and taken home, only 1 couple short,
after a roustering hunt and a fine finish
up to a grand season, with only 1 day's frost.